THE COUPLE CHECKUP

THE COUPLE CHECKUP

DAVID H. OLSON

AMY OLSON-SIGG

PETER J. LARSON

THOMAS NELSON
Since 1798

NASHVILLE   DALLAS   MEXICO CITY   RIO DE JANEIRO

Published in Nashville, Tennessee, by Thomas Nelson. Thomas Nelson is a registered trademark of Thomas Nelson, Inc.

Thomas Nelson books may be purchased in bulk for educational, business, fund-raising, or sales promotional use. For information, please e-mail SpecialMarkets@ThomasNelson.com.

Scripture quotations marked NIV are from the HOLY BIBLE: NEW INTERNATIONAL VERSION (NIV). © 1973, 1978, 1984. International Bible Society. Used by permission of Zondervan Bible Publishers.

ISBN 978-0-7852-3823-2 (tp)

Library of Congress Cataloging in Publication Data

Olson, David H. L.
　　The couple checkup / David H. Olson, Amy Olson-Sigg, Peter J. Larson.
　　　　p. cm.
　　Includes bibliographical references.
　　ISBN 978-0-7852-2827-1 (hardcover)
　　1. Man-woman relationships. 2. Couples. 3. Marriage. I. Olson-Sigg, Amy. II. Larson, Peter J.
III. Title.
HQ801.O57 2008
646.7'8—dc22   2008008581

Printed in the United States of America

13 14 15 QG 5 4 3

TO ALL COUPLES

May the love that brought you together

Nurture your relationship and your family

So you may better serve others and your community.

David Olson, Amy Olson-Sigg, & Peter Larson

CONTENTS

Preface   ix

ONE: Like a River Flowing   1

TWO: Discover Your Couple Strengths   15

THREE: Communication—The #1 Skill   33

FOUR: Conflict—An Opportunity in Disguise   55

FIVE: Finances—More than Money   79

SIX: Sex—Beyond the Birds and Bees   105

SEVEN: Roles—Traditions, Trends, and Teamwork   127

EIGHT: Spirituality—Live Out Your Values   147

NINE: Closeness and Flexibility—Map Your Relationship   163

TEN: Parenting—Creating a Balanced Family   191

ELEVEN: SCOPE Out Your Personalities   213

TWELVE: Achieving Your Goals   235

Notes   253
About the Authors   260

PREFACE

It is not so astonishing the number of things that I know,
as the number of things I know that aren't so.

—MARK TWAIN

We may know a lot about marriage research, but let's be honest: we do not know you personally. We do not know the details of your relationship that make it unique and, in some ways, different from anyone else's relationship. You and your partner are distinct individuals with your own personalities, your our own set of life experiences, and your own relationship history. You are at a certain stage in your relationship—dating, engaged, or married. Many of you are living together without being married, while others have been married for fifty years. Because of this, it would be very bold and perhaps misguided to throw recommendations at you as if we know what is best for your relationship. The alternative stance, and the one we choose to use, is to recognize that you are the expert on your own relationship. No one can know your relationship as well as you.

The problem with self-help books is they are about the book, not about you. Even the best psychological advice available, packaged in an entertaining, lucid, encouraging book, often has little lasting impact on a person's life. Why? Because advice is mass-marketed and generic, and couple relationships are specific and unique. No one, not even the most highly skilled psychotherapist, knows what you need better than you do. Unlike psychotherapy, where a good therapist is trained to understand context, find relational patterns, and help clients catalyze their own discoveries, self-help books miss the mark because they cannot know the reader.

The great author and psychiatrist Peter Kramer wrote an entire book pondering the existence of objective advice.[1] He contends that in order to help someone, it is necessary to really know the person. Without knowing, what appears to be advice is usually just the transmission of values enforcing cultural ideas of proper human behavior.

THE VOICES OF FIFTY THOUSAND "EXPERTS"

We have analyzed the marriages of over fifty thousand couples (one hundred thousand individuals) who answered extensive questions about a subject they know well: *their couple relationship*. We use the term "expert" because we trust that individuals have more expertise on their own relationship than anyone else could have. Yet we realize "expertise" is generally understood as both knowledge and *ability*. This is where the fun work of data analysis comes in handy. Based on how they described their marital satisfaction, we separated happy couples from unhappy couples and ran analysis on their *ability* to function in various capacities of life, from handling finances to dividing household tasks.

These results are compelling because they are based on the largest in-depth study of marriage ever conducted. Discoveries made by this study can be very helpful for couples who want to focus on behaviors and skills that will give them an edge in their goal to live on the happy side of this equation. For example, knowing that most happy couples work hard at having an equal relationship, compared to about half of all unhappy couples, may compel some to prioritize the work of maintaining equality in their relationship. There will be some couples, however, who do not fit into the percentages and averages and are very happy with an uneven balance of relational power and influence. For these couples, a research finding that is statistically correlated with unhappiness in most marriages may not be predictive of their own relational happiness. In this way they learn where they fit in and where they are like and unlike most other couples.

> "An unexamined life is not worth living."
>
> SOCRATES

EXAMINING YOUR OWN RELATIONSHIP

How is this book different from any other self-help book? Besides looking top-down from the national trends of fifty thousand couples, we will help you take a very personal look at your relationship by giving you access to an online "Couple Checkup." The online Couple Checkup evaluates the same areas of a relationship that form the contents of this book. This quickly personalizes the subject matter, enabling you to efficiently determine your strengths and those areas to improve in your relationship. You don't have to take the online Couple Checkup in order to benefit from this book—the results provided here, from our massive study, offer plenty of insight for your relationship. However, the Couple Checkup tailors the information, letting you quickly learn a great deal about the current state of your own relationship.

The online Couple Checkup and the contents of this book offer an external viewpoint based on theory, research, and a common language for describing relational phenomena. This outside perspective is not intended to replace you as the expert but to help you define and describe issues that can become clouded when you are immersed in your own subjective feelings about your relationship. Rather than handing over your power to an author who knows nothing about your relationship, you will be empowered to draw your own map based on your and your partner's strengths and preferences. Your road to a successful and happy relationship will be uniquely yours.

Get one free Individual Report at www.couplecheckup.com by using the voucher code provided on the inside book cover in the back of this book. This code also provides a significant discount on the purchase of the full Couple Checkup. Your partner can then take the Checkup that compares you and your partner and provides you a comprehensive Couple Checkup Report.

ONE

LIKE A RIVER FLOWING

You can never step into the same river,
for new waters are always flowing onto you.

—HERACLITUS OF EPHESUS

The sixth-century philosopher Heraclitus taught that nothing is permanent but everything is constantly changing. We cannot use our senses to perceive some changes because they are so gradual, yet they are real. Not only do our brains attempt to deny these truths when it comes to ourselves (our fight against aging being just one example) but we also want to believe that the people in our lives will remain stable and predictable. Our egos want to believe that relationships can be mastered, and will forever be glorious and meaningful. This is a common mistake that will eventually lead to disappointment.

YOUR RELATIONSHIP IS CHANGING TOO . . . DO YOU LIKE THE DIRECTION IT IS GOING?

A popular metaphor used to understand family and couple relationships is that of a river. Thinking about your family as a river emphasizes its long-term continuity, something that both reaches back in time and extends ahead into the future. More importantly, the river metaphor accentuates the ever-changing nature of families and relationships. On the surface a couple may look relatively stable, but deeper examination reveals "undercurrents" that change from moment to moment, altering the flow of the relationship. After all, couples are comprised of individuals who are affected by their own experiences and are changing their ideas and desires over time.

When Bob and Stephanie got married, their different views on education didn't seem like such a big deal. Like her family, Stephanie valued education. Bob, with his more entrepreneurial spirit, never felt suited in academia and dropped out after a year of college. Stephanie finished college and had just started a graduate program in political science when she learned she was pregnant with their first child. She continued on in her program after their daughter was born and started resenting Bob's flippant attitude toward education. He used to say, "A college degree isn't what it used to be. Everyone has a college degree nowadays." He was off chasing his dreams, which to Stephanie seemed to be more about the desire to make money than about building a life and family together.

Stephanie felt Bob didn't respect her work when he dismissed education and talked exclusively about making money. When Stephanie wasn't caring for their daughter, she was immersed in a world of like-minded people, who shared her enthusiasm and passion for the social policy issues they were studying. Bob and Stephanie had a lot of fun together and still felt relatively close, but Stephanie couldn't shrug the feeling that they were living in two different worlds. She wanted their daughter to have the opportunity to find her passion in the world through education, and she worried about the influence Bob's pessimistic view of education would have on their daughter.

Over time it is clear to see how Bob and Stephanie grew farther apart in their values. Using the river metaphor for their relationship, we see that as they move through life, they gather substance from different sources and join and blend with other "waters." These other sources naturally become more influential as couples transition into married life. In the early stages of their love and marriage, Bob and Stephanie felt cocooned in their love, with family and friends having a very peripheral role. But after several years of marriage, especially when children are involved, family and friends return as more central figures of influence. In the case of Bob and Stephanie, time and experiences with others solidified and enhanced differences that were already there.

We can easily recognize the effects of time on physical matter, and we act accordingly. For example, if you want your car to run and to last, you refuel, change the oil, replace brake pads, and so on. If you want your teeth to last your lifetime, you brush and floss daily, and you have a yearly dental checkup. If you want your body to remain healthy, you eat a variety of wholesome foods, exercise, get enough sleep, and have a medical checkup once a year.

- Would you drive your car one hundred thousand miles before getting an oil change?
- Would you go twenty-five years without a dental checkup?
- Would you have a physical exam only once in your lifetime?

Your relationship deserves a checkup too.

In contrast, although most couples report that being happily married is one of their priorities, regular couple checkups are rare. Especially considering the natural change that takes place in all things, it's surprising that many people are not intentional in knowing their partner and staying connected. The assumption is that a good relationship flows naturally. Whether one believes the source is God or just an organic flow from the wellspring of love and commitment, the fact is relationships often do seem to work well naturally.

But just as a river requires replenishment, so do relationships. Rivers lose substance to the earth through which they pass, to the air, and to those who draw water from them. Relationships also lose substance as they flow through time: from work demands, physical and mental health issues, and the countless other ways in which our time and energies are dissipated.

Replenishment is crucial to a happy partnership and can exist in a variety of forms, many of which may already be part of your relational connection—rituals, shared interests, a place of worship, family and friends, and so on. Reading this book with your partner and completing the exercises and Couple Checkup is a deliberate and concise way to replenish your relationship. Not only will you have the opportunity to customize the information and assimilate it into the uniqueness of your relationship, but you can also be assured that the questions are relevant in the first place.

Many of the ideas and insights into marriage and couple relationships in this book are based on research with thousands of couples who took the PREPARE-ENRICH couple inventory used by counselors and clergy. PREPARE-ENRICH has been taken by over 2.5 million couples nationally and internationally over the past twenty-five years. PREPARE-ENRICH contains twenty critical areas of a couple's relationship and consists of 165 key questions that couples answer. PREPARE is used to help premarital couples prepare for marriage. ENRICH helps married couples enrich their relationship. Using data from fifty-thousand married couples who took ENRICH, the content of this book is organized around a national survey of marriages that identifies what distinguishes happy couples from unhappy couples. (For more information on this, see chapter 2.

THE ROLE OF THE COUPLE CHECKUP AMID CHANGE

Wait a minute, you may be saying to yourself. *If all things are indeed changing, why gather information on a relationship* (in the form of a Couple Checkup) *if it is only going to change again?* This is a valuable and important question.

The point of the Couple Checkup is to get information about your relationship as a couple *at this moment.* Your answers to the questions are important now, but as the months and years pass, they will becomes less relevant as your relationship continues to change. To understand this analogically, imagine that you are looking at a photograph of your childhood home taken after a snowfall. Does it matter any longer that the sidewalk needed to be shoveled and there may have been disagreement over who would do the work? Of course not! It no longer matters, because it is no longer relevant.

So the way you answer the questions about your relationship matters—it matters a lot—but remember that it only reflects the present. Like that snapshot of your childhood home, it will someday represent a time in history. Even the most loving and nurturing relationships will be swept away by the current if ignored. Nothing ever remains the same forever . . . that is the process of life.

Relationships are living, growing, dynamic entities that require steady doses of nurturing, as well as periodic health checks. The failure to continuously nurture relationships is summed up in the all-too-common statements made by couples, such as, "I didn't realize he felt that way," or "I feel as though we do not know each other anymore." It is epitomized in the couple who "drifts apart," or after years of marriage (and often childrearing), feel as though they have lost the intimate bond they once had and are now just sharing living quarters.

What Exactly Is a "Couple Checkup"?

The Couple Checkup is an online assessment with approximately 120 questions about relationships. These questions cover between fifteen and twenty aspects of your relationship that research has identified as key areas for healthy relating. The questions are also designed to increase a couple's connection by encouraging them to talk about their relationship. The Checkup is based on the popular and highly successful PREPARE-ENRICH Program, which has been used by over sixty-five thousand clergy and counselors to help over 2.5 million couples prepare for marriage (PREPARE) and enrich their marriage (ENRICH).

Is the Couple Checkup Relevant to Us?

The Couple Checkup is designed to be relevant for couples who are dating or engaged, for couples who live together but are not yet married, and for married couples. Based on background questions that you answer about your relationship, the computer system will select relevant scales and questions for you to consider.

Dating couples. The characteristics that make for a good date are not necessarily the characteristics that make a good mate. The Couple Checkup, with its empirically based item relevancy, can help couples make good choices about their future. Seriously dating couples need objective feedback about their relationship quality before they commit themselves to an engagement and become caught up in the distractions of planning a wedding.

Amber and Justin had been dating for several years and were thinking about getting engaged when they took the Couple Checkup. Amber said:

> Taking the Couple Checkup with my partner just reinforced and validated the great connection we have and how strong our relationship is. Our results indicated that we were a "Harmonious couple" because we have many couple strengths. That was very reassuring. We learned we needed help in two areas: finances and how we handle conflict—which sparked some good discussion. Even though I was sure of our relationship before, I am even more confident that we are off to a great start.

Engaged Couples. It is important to realize that getting married is easy, but continually developing a healthy marriage is very challenging in our society. The United States is the most marrying-and-divorcing culture in the world. For the last ten years, the annual divorce rate in the United States has been about 50 percent, so marriage is a very risky social institution. But marriage continues to be the most popular voluntary choice that Americans make, as over 90 percent will marry at least once. There are 2.3 million marriages and 1.2 million divorces each year; and in about half of the marriages, one or both of the persons have been married before.

Premarital Couples. All premarital couples can benefit from the early detection of potential relationship issues by taking the Couple Checkup. Currently, only 35 to 40 percent of all engaged couples receive any premarital education. Premarital education has been shown to reduce divorce by 30 percent and to improve overall marital satisfaction.

Cohabiting Couples. This is another group that will find the Couple Checkup of value. The number of couples living together outside of marriage has dramatically increased over time. In 1970 only five hundred thousand couples were living together; the number rose to 3.7 million in 1996, and currently there are over 6 million cohabiting couples in the United States. Some of these couples will eventually marry, some will break up, and many will simply continue to live together.

Cohabiting couples are often unsure if they are going to get married, and if so, when that will occur. Sometimes one person is less interested in making the commitment to marriage than the other. One of the positive aspects of taking the Couple Checkup is that it will help couples look at how living together is impacting their relationship. It can also help them make a clearer decision about how they each feel about the relationship, and it will encourage them to discuss the next steps in their relationship.

Married Couples. The Couple Checkup is a relationship health checkup for married couples. It identifies their strengths and issues and stimulates relationship dialogue. It provides a way for couples to reconnect with one another while they talk about important issues. Research has found that married couples tend to seek marriage enrichment and counseling only after their marriage has been struggling for several years and one or both spouses have already considered divorce. Couples in this distressed state have lost sight of their relationship strengths and focus only on their conflicts and issues. The Couple Checkup can identify and address minor issues proactively, before they cause major problems in a marriage.

A couple married for several years took the Couple Checkup because they had ongoing issues that resurfaced again and again. After completing the questions online the wife said,

> The Couple Checkup was easy, quick to take, and the results were very helpful. Anthony and I were described as a "Conflicted couple," but that did not surprise me. In a way, I felt relieved to have things out on the table. Now we're doing our homework for our relationship and devoting a couple of evenings each week to talking about things that came up in the Checkup process. We are finally talking about important issues and not avoiding them. We've even talked about marriage counseling, but at the moment we feel good about just walking through these issues we avoided for so long.

THIRTY YEARS OF RESEARCH
AND MILLIONS OF COUPLES

We (David and colleagues) began designing assessment surveys for couples over three decades ago at the University of Minnesota. We constructed one of the first premarital assessments (PREPARE) in the late 1970s. This was followed by a marriage inventory (ENRICH) a couple of years later. These tools are now in their fifth edition and have been taken around the world by over 2.5 million couples (5 million individuals). Thirteen international offices have translated the PREPARE-ENRICH assessments into several different languages. The Couple Checkup, discussed in this chapter, is an adaptation of PREPARE-ENRICH, and a major difference is that the Checkup Report goes directly back to couples who takes it online.

Working with so many couples has allowed us to conduct many studies about couple relationships. Through our research, we have come to several important conclusions:

- **Each individual has their own unique opinion of their couple relationship.** One might assume couples in the same marriage or relationship would have similar opinions and levels of satisfaction about various aspects of their relationship. We quickly discovered, however, that couples often don't know how their partner really feels about things. There is "his" view of marriage and "her" view of their marriage, which often sounds like they are talking about different relationships. Our research has found that you can predict your partner's view of marriage only 25 percent of the time.

Marc thought everything was fine in his relationship. He and Mary had only been married two years, and while they'd had some arguments about the time he spent away on his hunting and fishing trips, it wasn't worth making a mountain out of a molehill. This was how he'd grown up. His mother never complained much, and his brothers' wives seemed to tolerate the annual trips without too much trouble. Mary had a different take on things. She felt abandoned and neglected in their relationship. She had no idea Marc would refuse to adjust his lifestyle after they were married. When they took their assessment, Marc was surprised to see how disconnected and dissatisfied Mary was. Until he saw it in black and white, he hadn't realized how much the issue had been eating away at Mary's opinion of their entire relationship.

- **Premarital couples tend to be overly idealistic about their relationship.** They believe that love will conquer all and the way they feel about one another will never change. The romance will never fade. Many engaged couples will gladly tell you they've met their soul mate, the one person in the world with whom they could possibly have a successful marriage. They are busy planning their wedding and all the details that go along with it. In the midst of this distracted and unrealistic mind-set, counselors face the challenge of helping these love-struck couples realistically look at some of the challenges that all married couples eventually face.

  In one of the first studies we conducted with premarital couples, the results demonstrated how rose-colored their worldview really was. A group in Minnesota had organized an eight-week educational series of lectures for about two hundred premarital couples. They invited several presenters to give very comprehensive talks about their areas of expertise (communication, finances, and so on). We were asked to organize a team of doctoral students to measure the impact of this program. We designed a rigorous study. After the eight-week lecture series came to an end, however, we were amazed to find no changes or improvements in the attitudes, knowledge, or behavior of the engaged couples. When we interviewed them later, they all felt the talks had been entertaining and had good information, but the vast majority of the couples felt the issues that were highlighted "really didn't apply" to them. Their idealism and rose-colored glasses prevented them from applying the information to their own relationships.

- **Married couples tend to lose sight of their relationship strengths.** As overly idealistic as premarital couples are, the trend among married couples is almost the opposite. When married couples start to struggle, their attitudes often begin to drift toward pessimism and a tendency to focus on the negative aspects of their relationship. In these cases, an assessment can help them identify some of their strengths and help them remember the good things that attracted them to one another in the first place.

When Ron and Barb showed up for counseling, they talked as if there was nothing left to save of their marriage. Even when prompted by their marriage counselor, they had a hard time identifying anything in their relationship they still felt good about. It was almost like a thick fog of negativity had settled on them and made it impossible to recognize anything of value. After taking the assessment, however, they were surprised to hear they had some strengths left in several areas of their relationship. Once their counselor began to point these out, they were able to begin the long process of reconnecting with and building on the positive aspects of their life together.

THE FLOW OF YOUR RELATIONSHIP

Like a river flowing over thousands of miles, couple relationships flow through the ever-changing passages of our lives. Any lasting relationship has changed (or surely will change) over time with the addition and subtraction of family members, in family and work responsibilities, with individual and relational crises that complicate life, and in personal emotional maturity. How a relationship sustains itself throughout the ebb and flow of life is what either adds or detracts from the volume and force of the relationship, determining its course and the ease with which it flows.

The old saying "You cannot receive what you do not give" describes the cyclical nature of giving and receiving. This book provides a medium for this exchange in the context of relationships, but ultimately *you* determine how much you will receive from it. Think of the book and the Couple Checkup report as input (and insight), with the output determined by your dialogue, participation, and attitude. So as you read through this book, enjoy the process, knowing you are contributing to the replenishment and vitality of your relationship, health, and happiness!

PREVENTION IS MORE POWERFUL THAN CURE

Prevention is emerging as a most important approach across a variety of disciplines (including dentistry, health care, global warming, terrorism, and more). The principle of prevention is often characterized as innovative, but is actually only a collision of common sense and knowledge. When you *know* that factories producing plastics are polluting the environment, it is easier and more practical to reduce the use of plastics, increase recycling, and use clean production methods than it is to clean contaminated systems later. *Knowing* that cigarette smoke is the leading cause of lung disease, it only makes sense to stop smoking rather than to try to cure diseased cells after they begin growing in your body.

Early detection and prevention are as important in relational problems as they are in health-care or environmental problems. Only after issues have been identified can they be dealt with and addressed. In fact, treating couples that wait too long to come for marital therapy is much like treating terminal cancer. The relationship has been so destroyed that it is very difficult to rebuild.

However, being more proactive in exploring ways to improve your relationship is a positive way to do damage control. Anyone who has been in a relationship longer than a year knows that relationships can be hard work. But that work can also be part of the most fulfilling and deeply rewarding experiences in your life.

By her third therapy session, a woman named Sandra told us, "I was so nervous about seeing a marriage therapist. I knew James and I had issues, but it felt safer to pretend that everything was fine. I was afraid that actually bringing up the issues would cause more problems and disrupt our marriage. So I kept telling myself it wasn't a big deal. . . . But once we finally started talking about what we each wanted and needed from our relationship, it was as if a new lightness came upon us . . . we laugh so much now, we can even joke about things that used to cause so much tension."

THE POWER OF YOUR ATTITUDE

Sandra and James have a secret weapon that often determines whether couples will deepen or damage their relationship: an attitude of being allies. Being allies means they will work together as a team. Human beings are unique in their self-reflection—their ability to make themselves and their own behavior the object of examination. This kind of introspection is bound to feel uncomfortable at times. A sense of humor, when appropriate, can alleviate some of this discomfort. It is also important to remember you are allies; you are collaborating to accomplish the same end result—a happier and more intimate relationship.

To get to this result, the attitude or approach you use can be more important than the actual words you say. The words we speak do not exist in a vacuum; there is always an emotional subtext. It is absolutely pointless to "say the right words" if the words exist in an atmosphere of insincerity or are used to abuse or cause harm.

I (Amy) have a friend I adore who thinks nothing of blabbing to others (even in my presence) things I have confided in friendship to him. He is a great storyteller, and I have also noticed part of what makes his stories so fun is how he embellishes details to jazz them up a bit. I do not believe he does this with mean or destructive intentions—it is just for effect. If you enter his world, you are fair game and likely will be a character in one of his hilarious tales.

I think this is a good example of attitude gone awry, because even though the embellishments are meant to be harmless and fun, there are definitely moments when being fodder in his stories can feel like a betrayal of trust. This type of friendship never deepens and grows. Even when he discloses pieces of his private world, I often choose not to reciprocate because I no longer feel safe. While this can be an appropriate response with acquaintances and friends, it would be an intimacy-breaker in marriage. True intimacy demands an openness that cannot exist unless you trust the sincerity of the other and feel confident that he or she will not cause injury by betraying your trust.

An atmosphere of trust must first exist (or be reestablished) in order for individuals to feel motivated to invest in their partnership. If one person feels emotionally unsafe or threatened, the relationship can only retract, never expand . . . and a day may come when there is little left of the relationship to build. An attitude of trust can do more to transform relationships than can the most perfectly expressed words. Edwin Friedman described the primacy of the emotional context in which language resides when he said, "People can only hear you when they are moving toward you, and they are not likely when your words are pursuing them . . . Attitudes are the real figures of speech."[1] Remember this idea as you read through this book and talk through your issues with your partner. It is imperative to join your partner in an attitude of being allies, rather than that of adversaries. There is so much to gain from this affirmative approach. As you will read about in the next chapter, the couple relationship is foundational in sustaining us as individuals, as families, and as members of the larger society. As allies, we work in concert to produce results that benefit everyone. As allies, we work together to adapt to an ever-changing environment. And only as allies can we reach a greater capacity for intimacy and love.

TWO

DISCOVER YOUR
COUPLE STRENGTHS

Focusing on strengths will empower
you and your relationship.

Once upon a time, a professor went into a first-grade classroom and asked, "Boys and girls, how many of you know how to sing?" All hands went up, waving enthusiastically. Then he asked, "How many of you are dancers?" Again, all hands went up, some children even jumped to their feet to demonstrate. Finally, the professor asked, "How many of you can draw a picture really well?" Once again, all the children raised their hands in the air. Later that day the professor went to his doctoral seminar and posed the same three questions. After asking, "How many of you can sing?" he saw a few shrugs, no hands, and no enthusiasm. "How many of you are dancers?" had the same response. And "How many of you can draw?" got one hand shyly raised, but without enthusiasm.

I (Amy) first heard this story ten years ago from my friend, a sports psychologist, Dr. Rob Gilbert, and it remains both my favorite and least favorite (or most upsetting) story. I love how poignantly it typifies the enthusiasm and confidence with which we seem to be born. At the same time, it unearths a disheartening reminder of what we lose as we age. I wish there were a way to inoculate young children from the self-criticism and social comparisons that eventually curb some of their enthusiasm.

Almost without exception, children are born confident in their strengths and abilities. Most newly dating and newly married couples share this optimism and confidence. Somewhere along the line couples, as well as schoolchildren, lose sight of their strengths and begin to notice their problems. This is surely a complex, multilayered issue but even a glance at the grading structure in schools shows this deficit-model set-up. When students receive an assignment or test back from a teacher, it is not what was done well that is circled in red pen, it is the errors. Likewise, 90 percent of research done on relationships and marriage is analyzed through the lens of problems or divorce. Very few studies have looked at what couples are doing right.

Branching from the principles of positive psychology, the "strengths perspective" is gaining popularity across a range of disciplines, including business and education. We would like this book to extend a strengths perspective into your couple relationship. Assessing and affirming your relationship strengths increase confidence and the ability to respond effectively to your own needs. Our behaviors and achievements are often derived from the resources we perceive to be available to us. If we come to think of ourselves as lacking in some way or riddled with problems, we will become overwhelmed and unmotivated. Strengths are a way to celebrate and affirm what we already do well, and they are a starting point for change.

Nonetheless, it is important to take an honest appraisal of possible barriers to intimacy in relationships. The focus of relationship problems in this book will be on issues we found to be common to all couples. The frequency of these issues among couples should normalize your own experience. We believe it is important for couples to see the global reach of relationship problems, because there are few sources providing realistic images of the actual issues most couples face. The lack of reality may be in part responsible for a disconnection between what we expect in relationships and the reality of our lives.

MARRIAGE IN THE TWENTY-FIRST CENTURY

A paradox exists these days: while individualism remains an encompassing characteristic of American life, familial and relational connectedness is revered and valued now more than any other modern time. Offices and playgrounds alike are often heard brimming with fathers and mothers swapping stories of their children and grandchildren. Fathers are more involved in their children's lives;

gender does not force a woman to choose between a family and a career. It seems we are approaching a better balance between the importance of the individual (within the context of community and family), equalized by a growing understanding of the impact couple- and family-life satisfaction can have on an individual's health, job productivity, and so on. And yet, paradoxically, all types of social problems (high divorce rates, incidence of child abuse, drug abuse, and depression) suggest a growing discontent within the lives of Americans.

Why does this apparently balanced ideology fail to render personal and familial bliss? One reason seems to be the way that American optimism permeates media and culture to the point that we are misled about the nature of real life. Our culture denies reality by tempting and manipulating us into believing that perfect (and fictional) role models are the ideal, that unpleasant experiences can be avoided, and that material success breeds contentment. We are bombarded with images of perfection as impetus to buy products. Our children are exposed to contrived and simplified television characters, which do not reflect our lives and portray unrealistic standards. We rarely hear about real problems that couples and families encounter and must work through.

Like a holiday snapshot, we often see only the positive aspects of couple and family life, and when the inevitable lows occur, it can easily feel less like "life" and more like a flawed system. A reprieve from good times feels like unhappiness. The normal ebb and flow of relationships feels painfully out of balance. In her book *Lies at the Altar*, Dr. Robin Smith gives a narrative of how the "lies" we are socialized to focus on before marriage distract from the truth, and that the secret to every great marriage is that it is lived in truth.[1] She elaborates that these "lies" are not conscious or deliberate; rather they are the result of unasked questions, unspoken needs, and a failure to truly see the relationship realistically.

THE PATH OF THE STRONG

Happy marriages are not marriages without obstacles; they are marriages where couples use obstacles as opportunities to grow in their partnership. There is often a certain amount of resistance for couples to address their "obstacles"—issues or things that cause your relationship to lose some of its vitality and energy. But not addressing the issues does not mean they do not exist. In fact, unacknowledged and unresolved, they become an even more powerful force in your relationship.

> "A block of granite, which is an obstacle on the path of the weak, becomes a stepping stone on the path of the strong."
>
> THOMAS CARLYLE
> (1795-1881)

These obstacles act as matter blocking a river, causing it to lose some of its purity and power as it moves downstream.

The Couple Checkup, that snapshot of your relationship at a particular moment in time, gives you the empowering tools you need to discover your strengths, define your issues (or growth areas), and draw on both to make better choices for your relationship. Your relationship deserves an honest analysis and is worthy of an endeavor of greatness. There is a tremendous payoff in happy relationships and marriages not only for individuals but also collectively for families and societies.

THE BENEFITS OF MARRIAGE

Recent research has found marriage to have many positive societal, familial, and personal benefits.[2] Married people tend to be healthier, live longer, have more wealth and economic assets, and have more satisfying sexual relationships than single or cohabiting individuals. In addition, children generally do better emotionally and academically when they are raised in two-parent families. Each year about 1.2 million couples get divorced in the United States, costing taxpayers an estimated $112 billion in federal and state expenditures.[3] Divorce, some argue, undermines the proper socialization of children, resulting in a disorganization and decrease in societal well-being. Let's look at some of the benefits of marriage in more detail:

- **Married people have a healthier lifestyle.** People who are married tend to avoid more harmful behaviors than do single, divorced, or widowed persons.[4] For example, married people have much lower levels of problem drinking, which is associated with accidents, interpersonal conflict, and depression. In general, married people lead a

healthier lifestyle in terms of eating, exercising, and avoiding harmful behaviors.

- **Married people live longer.** Married people live several years longer
  than do single, divorced, or widowed persons. This is often because
  they have the emotional support of their partner and more access to
  good health care.

- **Married people have more satisfying sexual relationships.** Over
  half (54 percent) of married males and 43 percent of married females
  are very satisfied with their sexual relationship. For cohabiting couples,
  about 44 percent of the males and 35 percent of females are very satisfied. The frequency of sex is also higher in married couples than in
  cohabiting and dating couples.

- **Married people are happier.** Married couples are happier than
  single men and women and report far less depression and anxiety
  than single, divorced, or widowed individuals. In addition, married
  women are much less likely to suffer abuse than cohabiting or never-
  married women. Married women also report less conflict and greater
  love and intimacy than their unmarried counterparts.

- **Married people have more wealth and economic assets.** Because
  married couples can pool their economic resources, they tend to be
  wealthier. In fact, the median household net worth for a married
  couple is $132,000, as compared to $35,000 for singles, $42,275 for
  widowed individuals, and $33,670 for divorced individuals.

- **Children generally do better in a two-parent home.** Children from
  two-parent homes tend to be more emotionally healthy and achieve
  better academically than children from divorced homes.[5] As teenagers, they are half as likely to drop out of school, they have higher
  grades, and they are less likely to have an unwed pregnancy. Children
  from two-parent homes also receive more parental attention (such as
  supervision, help with schoolwork, and quality time together) than

do children from single-parent homes. Children from single-parent homes have a much higher probability of growing up in poverty and experiencing a lower quality of life.[6]

- **Society benefits when children are raised within a family.** Communities with more married-parent families have lower rates of substance abuse and crime among their young people.[7]

ALL MARRIAGES ARE NOT EQUAL

Given all this great research on marriage, one may falsely conclude that marriage is the key factor to a better quality of life. But while more than 90 percent of Americans will marry at least once in their lifetime, almost 50 percent of these marriages will end in divorce. And for those who stay married, how happy are their marriages?

Studies indicate that many unhappy couples stay married. In examining different marriage types, researchers found that couples who have more traditional marriages (strong religious views, traditional role allocation, and high agreement in parenting) were *less happily married* than any other marriage type, yet they were *least likely to divorce*.[8]

In addition, when studying some marriages there is often not a consensus as to whether or not it is a happy union. Many times one partner is much happier than the other. This is demonstrated by the low correlation in marital satisfaction between spouses (r= −.56). This correlation means that if you know the satisfaction level of one marriage partner, you will only be able to predict the other partner's marital satisfaction 25 percent of the time.[9]

Statisticians and laypersons alike are familiar with the statement "statistics lie," and the statistics on divorce rates and marriage benefits are no exception. The issue is not that the statistics are false, but that, when presented alone, they create inferences that may not be true. For instance, when presenting valid research on how marriage benefits individuals, families, and society, the implication is that *all* marriages will reap these rewards. It obscures the possibility that some marriages may be unhappy or may contribute to dysfunction among individuals, families, and society. Likewise, when it is reported that 50 percent of marriages end in divorce, the implication is that the remaining half are happy. It obscures the fact that many couples remain married but are unhappy, or one person is happy and the other is not. For this reason, although there are valuable lessons provided by the statistics reported in this book, compare and contrast these research findings with your own experiences and preferences as you explore the status of your unique relationship.

HAPPY COUPLES VERSUS UNHAPPY COUPLES

The rationale for highlighting differences between happy and unhappy couples is found in the quote in the sidebar: we do not need to make all the mistakes ourselves—we can learn a lot from the experiences of others.

To identify the differences between happy and unhappy couples, we conducted a national study with over fifty thousand married couples. Based on their scores on a marital satisfaction scale, couples were classified as either "happily married" or "unhappily married." There were 20,675 happily married couples and 20,590 unhappily married couples. The middle group of about ten thousand couples were not included in the two groups because their marital satisfaction scales were either moderate, or one partner was high and one was low.

Through in-depth analysis using the marital inventory called "ENRICH," we found distinct differences between happily married and unhappily married couples. The five categories from ENRICH that discriminated the best between happy and unhappy couples were (in rank order): communication, couple closeness, couple flexibility, personality compatibility, and conflict resolution. We call these the "five keys to intimacy," and Figure 2.1 graphically represents these findings. It was possible to predict with 92 percent accuracy whether a specific couple was happy or unhappy just by analyzing their scores in these five categories.

> "Learn from the mistakes of others; you won't live long enough to make them all yourself."
>
> ANONYMOUS

FIGURE 2.1

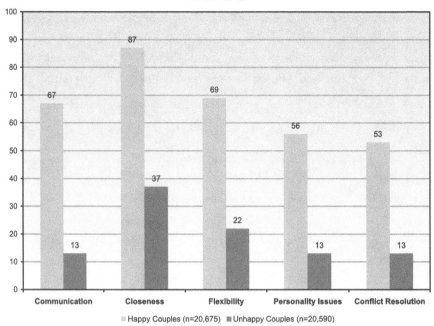

Happy Couples (n=20,675)   Unhappy Couples (n=20,590)

* PCA , or Positive Couple Agreement, measures the percentage of couple agreement that it is a positive relationship strength.

NATIONAL SURVEY DISCOVERS
NEW KEYS TO A HAPPY MARRIAGE

Why is it that some couples seem so happy, regardless of the situations, transitions, or circumstances they encounter in life? Are they simply well-matched individuals? Or are they doing something different than less-happy couples? What are their secrets?

Our national survey not only exposes the general categories which, when couples are in agreement, are most predictive of happy and unhappy couples but also reveals the detailed *items* within those categories that are most predictive of happily married couples. The remaining chapters are structured around these findings, with suggestions for improving your relationship based on the strengths of happy couples. Taking the Couple Checkup online will also provide you with an opportunity to see how your relationship compares with research findings across all of these key areas.

One of the major findings of the national survey was the discovering of new keys to a happy marriage: couple closeness, couple flexibility, and personality compatibility. Past studies of happy marriage have consistently emphasized two factors—communication and conflict resolution. While our study again found communication and conflict resolution to be important, the three new areas were significant new discoveries. In rank order of predicting a happy marriage, here are the five keys to intimacy:

1. Communication
2. Couple Closeness
3. Couple Flexibility
4. Personality Compatibility
5. Conflict Resolution

Not surprisingly, the area that most strongly distinguished happy couples from unhappy ones is *communication*. Happy couples appreciate the level of comfort provided by their partner, the ability to share important emotions and beliefs, their partner's listening and speaking skills, and the ability to communicate openly with their partner.

The second most important category distinguishing happy couples from unhappy ones is *couple closeness*. Couple closeness assesses the level of emotional connection experienced between partners and the degree to which they balance separateness and togetherness. Happy couples more often help each other, spend time together, express feelings of emotional closeness, and keep their relationship a top priority.

The third-ranking category, *couple flexibility*, reflects the capacity of a couple to change and adapt when necessary. Happy couples tend to share leadership more equally and are able to switch responsibilities and change rules when necessary. Chapter 9 provides an in-depth analysis and discussion of both couple closeness and couple flexibility.

Personality compatibility emerges as the fourth-ranked category for accurately distinguishing between happy and unhappy couples. Happy couples generally like the personality of their partner and do not feel their partner is trying to control them.

Conflict Resolution is the last of the five key categories that clearly differentiate between happy and unhappy couples. Happy couples agree that they are better able to resolve differences, talk openly with one another about issues, and understand one another's opinions and feelings in the midst of conflict resolution.

FIVE TYPES OF MARRIED COUPLES

One interesting way to assess marriage is to describe different types of marriages based on their level of satisfaction and their scores on the key areas of their relationship. Using our national survey, we found that there were five typical patterns or "types" of couples, ranging from very happy couples to the most unhappy. The most happy couple type we call Vitalized couples (18%) followed by Harmonious couples (24%). Conventional couples (17%) tend to fall between the happy and unhappy types of couples. The two couple types that are the most unhappy are Conflicted (22%) and Devitalized (19%) couples.

- **Vitalized Couples:** This is the happiest couple type, and these couples have strengths in most aspects of their relationships, including communication, conflict resolution, finances, and their sexual relationship. Only 14 percent of individuals in vitalized marriages have ever considered divorce.

FIGURE 2.2

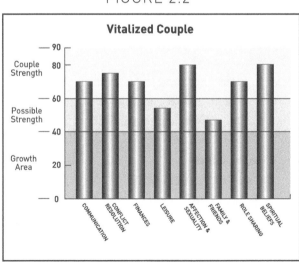

Susan and Jim have been married for over twenty years. In that time they have discovered that their passionate personalities that led them to fight with each other in their first decade of marriage have faded and now they appreciate and cherish each other more than before. They've learned to respect one another for the unique contributions each makes to the marriage, their parenting, and now grandparenting. They display their commitment by honoring each other in public (by speaking well of each other, for example) and in private (by listening and considering the opinions of the other). Their life together has had some valleys, including the threat of cancer, job loss, and a strong-willed child. But their strong commitment to each other and their communication and conflict resolution skills has carried them through.

- **Harmonious Couples:** These couples are very happy and have many strengths, but not as many strengths as Vitalized couples. Only 28 percent of the individuals in Harmonious marriages have ever considered divorce. They are satisfied with most areas of their relationship, particularly conflict resolution and their role relationship.

FIGURE 2.3

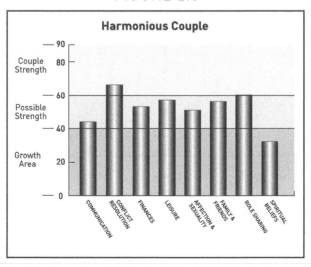

Carlos and Juanita make time for fun together each week and keep their relationship a priority. They share chores around the house and work together pretty well in deciding how to spend their money. They have learned to resolve issues before they become more serious, and this has really helped them grow closer together.

- **Conventional Couples:** These couples are generally happy and are called Conventional because they have more strengths in traditional areas, including agreement on spiritual beliefs, agreement on maintaining traditional roles, and a strong supportive network of family and friends. However, they have lower scores in areas involving more internal dynamics, including personality compatibility, communication, and conflict resolution. Over one-third (37 percent) of Conventional couples have considered divorce.

FIGURE 2.4

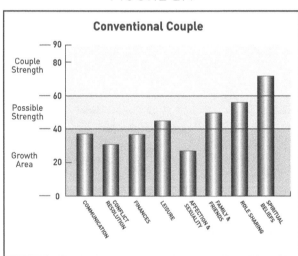

Stan and Carrie are somewhat happy in their marriage, but they sometimes feel isolated from each other. They have many shared friends, frequently surround themselves with extended family, and attend social functions. From the outside, this marriage looks better than it really is. Because the couple has few communication and conflict-resolution skills, they tend not to discuss their relationship and end up emotionally distant.

- **Conflicted Couples:** These couples are unhappy, and they have numerous growth areas and few relationship strengths. Nearly three-quarters (73 percent) of individuals in Conflicted relationships have considered divorce. They are called Conflicted because they disagree in many areas and have low scores in communication and conflict resolution. One of the most common types of couples to seek marital therapy is Conflicted couples because they often feel as if they have many unresolved issues.

FIGURE 2.5

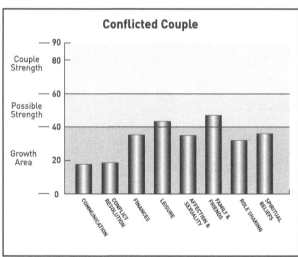

Donna and Frank are passionate people. They used to be passionate about each other, but when the infatuation of their courtship faded, their passion shifted toward trying to change one another. Now that they have been married for four years, they argue about many things. Whether the issue is money, sex, or each other's mother, they find themselves at odds much of the time. Donna complains to her girlfriends about Frank's temper and wonders if she married him too early in life. Frank questions whether Donna really loves him because she complains so much. Feeling like a failure as a husband only pushes him to spend more time at work, where he experiences success and feels more competent.

- **Devitalized Couples**: These couples are very unhappy and have growth areas in almost all aspects of their relationship. In over two-thirds (69 percent) of the couples, both spouses are dissatisfied, and about 90 percent of these individuals have considered divorce. They are typically very unhappy and have few strengths as a couple, although they might have had strengths earlier in their relationship. Conflicted and Devitalized couples are the two types that most often seek marital therapy or couple enrichment programs. A recent study found that a majority (93 percent) of couples attending a couple

FIGURE 2.6

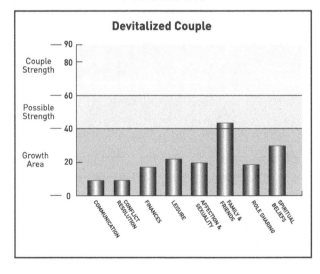

educational program called PAIRS were either Conflicted (34 percent) or Devitalized (59 percent). Only 7 percent of the couples enrolled in the PAIRS program were either Vitalized or Harmonious.[10]

> Kevin and Erica could be thought of as distant roommates. Well-practiced at shielding themselves from the negativity of the other, they've learned that avoiding each other is the lesser evil. They function separately as parents and feel isolated as partners. There is a great deal of stress in their relationship, and when they do speak, their sarcasm quickly takes over. They used to argue but have gotten worn down by the constant conflict. Lately, it just feels better to avoid each other.

WHAT IS YOUR COUPLE TYPE?

How do these findings about couple types apply to *your* relationship? First, as these couple types demonstrate, there are a wide variety of marriages in terms of both strengths and issues. Second, one of these types might be similar to the relationship you currently have with your partner. Third, these types can give you ideas about what you might want to change in your relationship. Fourth, you should consider what specific areas of your relationship you would like to improve and what type of marriage you might ultimately like to have with your partner.

Reflect on your couple type before moving on to other sections in this book. If discovering your couple type brings discouragement, remember that you can improve your relationship—that's the purpose of this book! Your couple type is where you are *today*, and we will give you ideas about how to improve your relationship going forward.

KNOWLEDGE IS POWER

These findings clearly demonstrate that some types of marriages have significantly more relationship strengths than other types. As you continue reading the next chapters, refer to your personalized Couple Checkup to identify your strengths

> "You can't stop the waves, but you can learn to surf."
>
> JON KABAT-ZINN

and to see which specific issues you and your partner need to discuss.

Each of the following ten chapters follows a similar format. First, differences between happy and unhappy couples are briefly outlined. Common problems are then discussed—these are the specific issues within each category that research demonstrates pose the most challenges for all couples. You can then compare these to your own results from the Couple Checkup.

Simply understanding the differences and obstacles in our relationships removes some of the power they have over us. Awareness generates in us the ability to maneuver more intelligently, perhaps by confronting the challenges that these issues pose rather than tripping over them. Knowledge *is* power—at the very least we discover something about ourselves and our relationships; we have more degrees of freedom to change the story, if that is what we desire. The following little parable humorously illustrates how knowledge can change your direction.

AUTOBIOGRAPHY IN FIVE SHORT CHAPTERS

By Portia Nelson

I. I walk down the street. There is a deep hole in the sidewalk. I fall in. I am lost . . . I am helpless. It isn't my fault. It takes forever to find a way out.

II. I walk down the same street. There is a deep hole in the sidewalk. I pretend I don't see it. I fall in again. I can't believe I am in the same place. But it isn't my fault. It still takes a long time to get out.

III. I walk down the same street. There is a deep hole in the sidewalk. I see it is there. I still fall in . . . it's a habit. My eyes are open. I know where I am. It is my fault. I get out immediately.

IV. I walk down the same street. There is a deep hole in the sidewalk. I walk around it.

V. I walk down another street.[11]

WALKING DOWN ANOTHER STREET

We want to encourage you to redefine your relational obstacles as opportunities within the course of your relationship. Physical obstacles, such as a block of granite, and a metaphorical obstacle, such as a disagreement, have common consequences. Each produces a slowing-down response, which is so important, perhaps even more so in today's fast-paced technological age. This slowing-down process is a natural and helpful response to stress. We need the time to experience our feelings, identify our thoughts, reflect on their meanings, and discern the wisdom of our next steps.

There is a direct correlation between actions and outcome. We control our actions; therefore, we control our lives. A problem in a relationship calls attention to issues that need to be addressed the same way that an illness is your body's way of telling you to rest and take care of yourself. A relationship problem communicates something about the needs of the individuals involved. Knowing these issues gives you a picture of your relationship now, and addressing them paves the way for improving these areas in the future.

When we know how we relate we can choose to become more intentional with our actions in the future. This book is about helping you take action and make better choices—choices based on knowledge about relationships, particularly your own. Because, as Oprah Winfrey is fond of saying, "When you know better, you'll do better." Let's begin.

THREE

COMMUNICATION— THE #1 SKILL

Two monologues do not make a dialogue.

—JEFF DALEY

HOW HAPPY COUPLES COMMUNICATE

One goal of the national survey is to identify the strengths of happy couples— learning from couples who are happily married. Experience is undeniably the best teacher. Other people's hindsight can certainly become your foresight. With this principle in mind, let's briefly review the results from our national sample of married couples. To discover the communication issues that distinguish happily married and unhappily married couples, we will review the major findings (see Figure 3.1).

The study espouses communication as a major gauge of marital happiness. Spouses in happy marriages are six times more likely than those in unhappy marriages to agree that they are very satisfied with how they talk to each other. These spouses are significantly more likely to feel understood by their partners, and they find it much easier to express their true feelings than their unhappy counterpoints do. A majority of happy spouses believe that their partners are good listeners, whereas only a small percentage of unhappy spouses feel this way. And almost four-fifths of happy spouses agree that they do not make comments to put each other down, compared to only one-fifth of unhappy spouses.

FIGURE 3.1
Communication Strengths of Happy Couples vs. Unhappy Couples

Percentage in Agreement	Happy Couples	Unhappy Couples
Communication Issue		
1. I am very satisfied with how we talk to each other.	95%	15%
2. My partner understands how I feel.	79%	13%
3. I find it easy to express my true feelings to my partner.	96%	30%
4. My partner is a very good listener.	83%	18%
5. My partner does not make comments that put me down.	79%	20%

THE COMPLEXITY OF COMMUNICATION

Communication is a word embedded in its own mystique. Everyone seems to understand what is meant by *communication*, yet conceptually and functionally it is very complex. These complexities can be studied in depth; in fact, there are undergraduate and graduate degrees dedicated solely to the study of communication. For the purpose of this book, *communication* is defined as "the dynamic process through which people try to convey meaning to one another."

Since language is the form of communication specific to human beings, people often focus primarily on words when thinking about communication. It is essential to remember that communication often has less to do with the words we use and more to do with their underlying meaning. Communication involves words (content) plus the relationship (how it is said). Think about the words "I can't believe you bought a new puppy without my knowing!" Without contextual awareness and without hearing voice inflection, how

> It's not *what* you said; it's *how* you said it.

well do we understand the meaning behind this message? Is this a five-year-old's squeal of delight or an irate wife's message to her husband?

YOU CANNOT *NOT* COMMUNICATE

To further complicate communication is the fact that it is always happening. If we accept that communication is the act of exchanging information, then we must acknowledge that even silence conveys information. The classic strategy of giving someone the silent treatment is not intended to be a refreshing reprieve from the exchange of words but a source of punishment to the receiver.

Many couples are fond of saying, "We are not communicating," when what they really mean is that the intended outcome of the sender did not occur. For instance, Mom and Dad may tell their daughters Britney (15) and Taylor (17) that Sunday is a family day, with the intention of creating family closeness. Britney and Taylor will spend Sundays with family instead of friends, and yet they may spend the day sulking or giving their parents the silent treatment. Even though Sunday is a family day, the family may not feel as though they have achieved their purpose—increasing their sense of togetherness. The intended outcome's not happening does not mean that communication did not happen. In fact, even if Britney and Taylor were to reject the idea of family day altogether, it would not mean communication wasn't taking place.

COMMUNICATION IS A KEY TO INTIMACY

The way we communicate constitutes our relationships and our lives. The ability to share our thoughts and feelings with others is vital in how relationships are formed and maintained. In fact, communication skills become even more important as the level of intimacy in a relationship increases. We clearly expect our partners to listen with more interest and speak with more sensitivity than we would expect from an acquaintance. Yet strangers often listen more carefully to us than our partners.

> "Communication is not only the essence of being human, but also a vital property of life."
>
> JOHN A. PIERCE

Communication is vital because it is the link to every aspect of our relationships. The outcome of discussions and decisions about finances, children, careers, religion, and even the expression of feelings and desires will all depend on the communication styles, patterns, and skills you have developed together.

Communication has the power to bring couples together and the means to push couples apart. It has the capacity to convey anger or forgiveness, happiness or sadness, love or concern. The willingness and ability to communicate contribute greatly to the health and happiness of a relationship. The good news is that communication is a learned skill; something that can be taught and practiced.

COMMON COMMUNICATION PROBLEMS

> "It is a luxury to be understood."
>
> RALPH WALDO EMERSON

Communication and intimacy are interrelated. Couples, especially unhappy spouses, are often heard to complain, "We don't communicate." But it is impossible not to communicate. In fact, the absence of conversation, physical contact, smiles, or self-disclosure "communicates" a lot about the feelings people have toward each other. Our national survey of fifty thousand married couples identified specific communication issues that are problematic for married couples.

FIGURE 3.2
Top Five Communication Problems for Couples

Communication Issue	Percentage of Couples Having Problem*
1. I wish my partner were more willing to share his/her feelings.	76%
2. I sometimes have difficulty asking my partner for what I want.	69%
3. My partner often does not understand how I feel.	65%
4. My partner often refuses to discuss issues or problems.	64%
5. My partner makes comments that put me down.	62%

One or both partners indicated this was an issue for them.

What is striking in these findings is the high percentage of all couples that agree on several very common problems in communication with their partner. Notice how the majority of all married couples wish their partners would share their feelings more often. Many spouses have difficulty asking their partner for what they want, do not feel understood, and feel that their partner will not discuss issues with them. Still another common problem with married couples is feeling put down by their partner. So it appears that most couples agree on communication problems in their marriage.

Now refer to the Communication section of your Couple Checkup. Do you share many of the common problems for married couples? Pinpoint the discussion items you could improve upon and focus on those as you read through the chapter.

MAKING ASSUMPTIONS OFTEN FAILS

> "Your assumptions are your windows on the world. Scrub them off once in a while or the light won't come in."
>
> ALAN ALDA

One pattern couples fall into that may contribute to feelings of being misunderstood is the tendency for spouses to assume they know each other. While couples are dating, each individual is often asking the other questions and talking about their life experiences, thoughts, and feelings. But the longer two people are together, the more they assume they know each other and so may neglect to ask questions and continue learning about each other.

But remember the river metaphor? Although your partner may appear the same this week as they did last week, they will have been affected by a week of reflecting and reacting to life's experiences. The most drastic changes are yet to occur and are not physical, but emotional, mental, and spiritual. So to assume that you know your partner's thoughts and feelings today based on the past can lead to a decrease in communication, which then results in less sharing and mutual understanding.

THE NEGATIVE SHIFT OVER TIME

Engaged couples and couples in the early stages of marriage tend to look for the positive qualities in their partners and either overlook negative qualities or regard them as unimportant. Slowly and subtly, however, this pattern often shifts. Partners who have been married for many years tend to be more focused on the negatives in the other person and in the relationship. As found in our survey, about two-thirds of married individuals receive negative "put-down" comments from their partners.

Because we tend to see only what we are focused on, a negative focus can create even more problems. For example, have you ever bought a new car and suddenly noticed that a lot of people are driving the same car? In reality, there are not more people driving that same model of car than were before you purchased it, but your focus has changed so that you now notice that car more. We tend to find what we are looking for—what we are focused on. Thus, in your marriage if you are focused on the negatives and you share those negatives with your partner, you will come to believe that there are more negatives than positives in the relationship.

John Gottman and his colleagues have conducted longitudinal studies on more than two thousand married couples and found that happy couples on average have five times as many positive interactions and expressions as negative interactions and expressions.[1] Gottman refers to this 5:1 ratio as "the magic ratio." What this means is that stable couples do not necessarily have less negativity in their relationship, but the negativity is greatly outweighed by positive feelings and actions. Gottman also points out that anger is harmful most often when it is expressed along with criticism.

HEARING IS NOT LISTENING

The one communication skill that is paramount to good communication is listening. Listening is not the same as hearing. Hearing is an involuntary physical act of sound waves impinging upon the ear. It is passive; it requires only healthy ears. We can hear someone talking without listening to them. Listening requires cultivation. Conscious thought must be given to understand what is said. It is also important to notice the things that get in the way of really listening to our partner, including the internal distractions that occupy our minds.

One such inner distraction—and a common listening mistake people make—is preparing a response while the other person is still talking. If you are planning your response or deciding whether you agree or disagree instead of listening attentively, the accuracy of the speaker's message will be greatly diminished. You may subordinate any of the speaker's ideas that do not fit within your own paradigm. What you interpret as agreement with the other may actually be a force-fit of their ideas into your pre-existing beliefs, rather than a true understanding of what is actually being said.

Another common listening mistake is listening defensively. Defensiveness is a natural response to feeling attacked, stereotyped, or generalized. Hearing a statement that begins with "you always . . ." universally results in defensiveness in the receiver. Nobody wants to be reduced to the idea that she *always* behaves a certain

> "It seems rather incongruous that in a society of super-sophisticated communication, we often suffer from a shortage of listeners."
>
> ERMA BOMBECK

way. While these feelings of defensiveness may be justified, they can also get in the way of objective and effective listening. Defensiveness can interfere with your ability to really interpret and understand the person speaking to you.

An important listening skill that minimizes defensiveness and internal distraction is *paraphrasing*. A paraphrase is your own interpretation of ideas expressed by someone else. It is simply restating what you hear, on both the content level (ideas) and the feeling level (affect and emotion). The following example demonstrates the two levels of content and feeling in paraphrasing.

Patricia: "You've been gone every night this week!"

Rob: "I *have* been working late every night this week [restating the idea]. It sounds like you are upset about this [restating the feeling]."

Often feelings need to be extrapolated from tone of voice, gestures, expressions, or context. One of the payoffs of paraphrasing is that if feeling or content are not accurately paraphrased, the other person has the opportunity to clarify further. This process often illuminates deeper understanding for both people involved. For example, in the above example, once Rob names the feeling he observes, Patricia can agree or disagree. She could respond in the way that clarifies how she feels without being negative.

Patricia: "Well I am not really upset. And I understand that you have been working on a big project at work. I just miss having dinner together."

Instead of this scenario between Patricia and Rob being accusatory and defensive, paraphrasing has forced a deeper understanding. By Rob not only restating the content but also dealing with the feelings beneath the words,

Patricia is more likely to feel understood and appreciated. What could have been a tense exchange instead becomes an almost-tender moment.

Practice paraphrasing with your partner, especially when you are having problems. It may feel awkward at first, because it is not how people normally talk to one another. It slows down the communication process, but this is purposeful. Slowing down by paraphrasing allows you to make your intent clear, to minimize defensiveness, and to avoid the communication pitfalls that stem from misunderstanding.

WHAT'S YOUR COMMUNICATION STYLE?

Every time we communicate with someone we use a style—a preferred way for both communicating *with* others and interpreting communication *from* others. Four major styles of communication in relationships include: passive, aggressive, passive-aggressive, and assertive. The healthiest and most effective style is assertiveness. The following description of each communication style can help you identify your own and your partner's communication style and give you an incentive to learn and practice assertive communication.

Passive Communication

A person with a passive communication style does not express their honest feelings or desires. They will defer to others' opinions instead of voicing their own; saying things such as "I don't care," "It doesn't matter to me," or "You decide." Passive people want to avoid conflict, and may believe that their rights are not as important as those of other people. Passive communication stems from low self-esteem and is often used to avoid hurting other's feelings, to avoid conflict, or to avoid being criticized. While it is done with good intentions in mind ("I didn't want to hurt them," "I was afraid I'd say the wrong thing," and so on), passive communication is not good for an individual or a relationship. A passive person often allows their own rights to be violated, which ultimately leads to feelings of not being understood or appreciated.

Aggressive Communication

Someone with an aggressive communication style behaves oppositely than a passive individual. A person with an aggressive style demands that his opinions, desires, and needs are met, often at the expense of others' rights. They rarely defer to others, essentially sending a message of "What I want is more important than what you want." Aggressive communication, like passive communication, also stems from low self-esteem and is used in order to "win" or to be right at any expense. An aggressive communicator tries to dominate others by criticizing or blaming. They have a low tolerance for frustration, interrupt frequently, and do not listen well. When people communicate aggressively, they are often trying to hold other people responsible for their own feelings. Aggressive communication leaves one person feeling hurt or invalidated. The aggressor may get their way, but only by destroying trust and intimacy within the relationship.

Passive-Aggressive Communication

Someone with a passive-aggressive communication style will forfeit their rights and desires initially but then will subtly convey anger or seek vengeance later. Like passive communicators, a passive-aggressive communicator's goal is to avoid conflict, but they will then use tactics to make the other party wish they had seen things their way. The typical pattern is to behave passively to a person's face, then become aggressive when the person is not around. The message is, "I will appear cooperative, but you should really do things my way." Passive-aggressive behavior stems from low self-esteem. People who use this style are often sarcastic and have a hard time acknowledging that they use this style.

Assertive Communication

A person with an assertive communication style expresses his feelings, rights, and desires without violating the rights of others. Assertiveness is the middle ground between passivity and aggression. It is asking clearly and directly for what you want, while being considerate to others. The goal is to find a solution while communicating respectfully. The message is, "Both of our needs and desires matter, so let's find a solution that meets both." Assertiveness stems from high self-esteem; it acknowledges personal responsibility and respect for self and others. Assertive communication is a means of relating authentically with others, which fosters a sense of connectedness to others.

HOW COMMUNICATION STYLES
AFFECT YOUR RELATIONSHIP

The communication style a couple develops influences the level of intimacy and closeness they will have. Figure 3.3 lists communication styles and their associated relationship styles, outcomes, and intimacy levels. For example, the passive couple is typified by not asking for what they want, and so partners usually will not get what they want. The result is a devitalized relationship with a low level of intimacy. When one partner is aggressive and the other is passive, the aggressive partner tends to dominate the relationship, which also results in low levels of intimacy. And when both partners use an aggressive style, their relationship is likely to be conflicted with low intimacy.

In contrast, assertive communication makes it more likely that partners will get what they want, increasing the happiness, authenticity, and intimacy in their relationship. It is important, however, that both individuals are assertive. If one partner is assertive and one is passive, the relationship will be frustrating for both, resulting in lower intimacy. If one partner is assertive and one is aggressive, the relationship may be confrontational, also resulting in lower intimacy.

FIGURE 3.3
Communication Patterns and Intimacy

Person A Communication Style	Person B Communication Style	Relationship	Who Wins	Level of Intimacy
Passive	Passive	Devitalized	Both lose	Low
Passive	Aggressive	Dominating	1 wins, 1 loses	Low
Aggressive	Aggressive	Conflicted	Both lose	Low
Assertive	Passive	Frustrated	Both lose	Low
Assertive	Aggressive	Confrontational	Both lose	Low
Assertive	Assertive	Vitalized	Both win	High

Heather and I (Peter) were just engaged when we first slipped into one of these negative communication patterns. I was in graduate school in California, and Heather had traveled from the Midwest that summer to visit and look at places we might live after our wedding that fall. I had come across an option that I was very excited about. It was on a little ranch in the foothills and I could work as a grounds keeper and take care of two horses in exchange for a free apartment. Since I knew our finances would be tight, I was immediately tempted to commit to this option (even before Heather had seen the property).

When she arrived for her visit, she had a different take on the opportunity. First of all the "apartment," referred to as "the barn," was nothing more than a finished space over an actual barn that was used for equipment, feed, and tools. The carpet in the second-level living space was dark brown, complemented by dark, paneled walls. The whole space was one large room. Worst of all, the kitchen area was about the size of a closet, and it featured miniature appliances. This was not her vision of where we would establish our first home together.

As Heather remembers it now, she knew immediately that the situation did not appeal to her, but she did not want a conflict since she knew I was so excited about the "free" living option. I could tell she wasn't that excited about it, but I saw her hesitancy as something I should overcome by convincing her of the merits of the situation. In the end, her passivity gave way to my aggressive negotiating.

It was not long after we moved in that we heard rats scraping in the ceiling and walls at night. Living in the foothills of Los Angeles, I had not anticipated hearing screaming coyotes hunting rabbits at night, nor did I expect to find rattle-snakes searching out the rodents in and around "the barn." And we were told we could not return home for the holidays: I had to stay and feed the horses. It was at that point I went to Heather with my head hung low, suggesting that we move as soon as possible. She was gracious about the situation and never said, "I told you so." Looking back, my biggest regret is not having made a poor choice in living arrangements but letting our first major decision as a couple be one in which I failed to listen to my wife because I aggressively pushed to "win" the decision. It was not long before my win-lose approach proved to be a lose-lose.

CREATING INTIMACY THROUGH COMMUNICATION

An important outcome of having a relationship characterized by the five communication strengths of happy couples is emotional safety. When an individual feels good about her communication, feels understood, can express her true feelings, and knows she will be heard and not criticized, that individual is experiencing an emotional environment in which it is safe to be open and real. When two individuals feel the freedom to be real with one another, intimacy and connection become natural by-products of their freedom to be authentic with one another.

On the other hand, when a person doesn't feel understood or listened to and is aware that he may be put down when he tries to express his true feelings, he is very likely to build an emotional wall to protect himself. That type of emotional environment does not feel safe, nor does it foster openness that might lead to increased connection or intimacy.

The following communication strategies are skills that can be learned. But consider how each of these approaches fosters safety in the emotional environment in which your communication takes place. One might suggest that all of the following communication skills and suggestions are really about increasing emotional safety so dialogue can be productive rather than threatening.

Meaningful Dialogue

Every living thing needs nurturing and attention. If you want to plant a tree and have it thrive, you don't simply set the tree in the yard and hope for the best. Instead, you dig a hole, carefully place the sapling in it, and surround it with good soil. You add fertilizer and water and begin daily monitoring its health and growth.

It is the same with your couple relationship. Your relationship needs attention on a daily basis, which can be as simple as five minutes of meaningful dialogue. The focus of this daily dialogue should be on your feelings about each other and your life together. So, set aside five minutes per day and fifteen minutes on the weekends to discuss the following:

- What did you most enjoy about your relationship today?

- What was dissatisfying about your relationship today?

- How can things be made better for each of you?

Couples typically resist discussing negative feelings because they do not want to create problems or arguments. But what really happens when issues are not discussed is the opposite. As in an untended garden, ignored feelings have a weed-like way of taking over, of growing up through ever-widening cracks. Eventually, they may lead to resentment, disinterest, and a lack of desire to repair the relationship. Couples who wait too long to discuss things that are bothering them are at risk of becoming gradually apathetic toward one another. Apathy becomes a protective layer between vulnerability and the perception of being devalued.

If you sense that your partner has become less interested in communicating with you, it feels less wounding to convince yourself that you don't care, rather than to tell yourself you are becoming less desirable in his or her eyes. This may be self-protective, but it is dangerous to a relationship—after all, the opposite of love is not hate; it is apathy. So, do not hesitate to include the satisfying and the dissatisfying aspects of your day in your daily dialogue. Know that taking part in this simple dialogue is one way to tend to your relationship as you would any living thing you want to thrive.

Self-Disclosure

Another way to create intimacy in your relationship is through self-disclosure. Self-disclosure is the revelation of deeply personal information about yourself, things that most people do not know about you. By sharing your innermost thoughts and private feelings, you bring your relationship to a deeper level.

Self-disclosure creates an environment of mutual trust, which benefits both individuals in a relationship. When you share your thoughts and dreams with someone special, you not only reveal yourself to that person but also learn about yourself. It feels good to be open, and it also feels good to have someone confide in you.

Self-disclosure has a reciprocal effect as well. When we confide in others, they increasingly will confide in us. Studies show that married couples typically share more negative feelings and fewer positive ones. However, those couples who are most happy in marriage willingly share both positive and negative feelings. Whereas silence isolates us, self-disclosure connects us.

Assertiveness and "I" Statements

Two important communication skills used often by happily married couples are assertiveness and "I" statements.

An analysis of personality characteristics using the PREPARE-ENRICH couples' program showed that people who have high scores on assertiveness also tend to be low in avoidance and do not feel controlled by their partners. They also liked their partners' personalities, felt good about their communication, and liked how they resolved couple conflict. So being assertive had a very positive impact on how a couple saw their relationship.

An "I" statement is a declaration about your feelings. They are important because they communicate facts without placing blame and are not likely to promote defensiveness in the receiver. Since "I" statements do not communicate blame, they are more likely to be understood. In contrast, "You" statements create defensiveness because they sound accusatory. For example, think about how you would respond to the following:

> "The problem with communication is the illusion that it has been accomplished."
>
> GEORGE BERNARD SHAW

"You" statement: "You are so inconsiderate to me in front of your friends!"

"I" statement: "I feel hurt when you put me down in front of your friends."

Other "you" statements to avoid include "you always . . ." ("you're always late") and "you never . . ." ("you never think about anyone except yourself"). "Always" and "never" are one-dimensional accusatory words that diminish the other person, impelling him or her to deny everything you have said. Afterall, it would be quite unlikely that somebody would always or never act in a certain way.

ACTIVE LISTENING USING PARAPHRASING

The "illusion" that communication has happened, which George Bernard Shaw refers to in the quote in the sidebar, is often at the root of couple squabbles. As I (Amy) write these words, I am chuckling to myself as I recall such an illusion that happened less than twenty-four hours ago. The battery was dead on my car, and my husband helped me push the car out of our garage before he jump-started it with his car. It was already eleven o'clock on a Monday night, but I knew I needed to drive it around a bit to recharge the battery. After noticing it was low on gas, I first drove it to a corner gas station, and then reflexively shut the engine off as I got out to refuel.

Of course, the car would not restart again. I was happy I had a phone with me, and I called my husband to let him know my battery needed another jump. We live within equal distance of two gas stations, and I told him I was at the Amoco. I was completely under the illusion that he understood where I was, but I soon learned the station I was at was no longer an Amoco. My husband went to the other gas station to look for me! Luckily we both had a good sense of humor about this little situation, but it is easy to see how it could be otherwise, particularly if we had been under stress or on a deadline.

One of the most distinguishing characteristics between happily married couples and unhappily married couples is whether or not individuals feel understood. Paraphrasing, a form of active listening, allows feelings, as well as the actual content of your message, to be understood. By verbally feeding back what you hear, you clarify that the message has been accurately received and interpreted. The goal of paraphrasing is to clarify and increase mutual understanding. It can be as simple as restating the exact content you heard from the speaker, or it can offer or ask for further clarification. For my husband and I, paraphrasing could have gone like this:

> **Amy:** I am at the Amoco station.
> **Daniel:** You are at the Amoco station. Is that the one next to the Italian restaurant?
> **Amy:** No, I am at the other one—the one next to Caribou Coffee.

Most people are quite good at this type of paraphrasing; it is only with feeling-laden conversations that we get misled by our own agendas, which is often protecting or defending ourselves. For example, my husband could have been upset when I called and said something like, "This is turning out to be such a hassle. Why couldn't you wait until morning to get gas for your stupid car anyway? I was hoping to be in bed by now!"

I could then choose to react to his comment by defending my decision, or I could paraphrase by acknowledging the content and feeling of his message. The defensive response might be, "It's too late now—just get your butt up here! And anyway, you get up so early you probably would have to leave for work without helping, and I would be stranded." That defensive reaction easily slips into subtle undertones of "your leaving early to work is a problem and, by the way, you are not very considerate either."

But the potential for argument and bringing up past irrelevant events is clear when we become defensive and do not limit ourselves to rephrasing content and feeling. An out-of-control, overstressed, off-task couple could quickly take this little exchange from "I need another jump" to "You have the luxury of leaving early for work while I have to get the children off to school and daycare before I can go to work!"

Paraphrasing keeps the conversation on the task at hand and increases emotional safety, preventing couples from going down the road of no return (bringing up the past, defending their position, and so on). Imagine the following conversation:

My husband: "This is turning out to be such a hassle! Why couldn't you wait until morning to get gas for your stupid car? I was hoping to be in bed by now!"

Me: "I know—it *is* a hassle. And I know you have to get up early, so thanks, honey."

The simplest and most important thing we can give someone is our attention, and active listening through paraphrasing is one of the most basic and powerful ways to stay on task and prevent problems while still connecting to others.

DAILY COMPLIMENTS

Giving your partner at least one compliment each day may sound simplistic, but it can have a remarkable effect on your relationship. We often are more inclined to compliment acquaintances or co-workers than our spouses. Giving at least one daily compliment to your partner will help you focus on your strengths as individuals. It will also highlight the positive qualities that initially attracted you to each other. Notice in Figure 3.1 that 80 percent of unhappy couples feel that their partner puts them down.

Instead of making comments to put your partner down, make compliments to boost them up! Think of the two of you as a team. Supporting your partner personally will inevitably benefit you too. Daily compliments will prevent your relationship from becoming routine and will make it more mutually satisfying. Receiving a compliment not only makes you feel good but it also makes you feel good about the person giving the compliment.

Compliment your partner on his physical attributes, things she says and does, or what he stands for. Women and men both love to be complimented, and doing so demonstrates that you notice and appreciate them. Remember, what you give to your partner is what you will receive in return.

CHECK-IN PROCESS

Where are you *now*? (Identify and discuss your results.)

1. Review the Couple Checkup *individual* results. How satisfied were each of you in this area?

_____

_____

2. Review the Couple Checkup *couple* results. Was communication a strength or growth area?

_____

_____

3. Discuss your agreement items (your strengths).

_____

_____

Where would you like to be? (Discuss issues.)

1. Review the discussion items in your Couple Checkup report.
2. Choose one issue you both want to resolve.
3. Share how you each feel about the issue.

How do you get there? (Develop your action plan.)

1. Brainstorm a list of ways to handle your communication problems.
2. Agree on one solution you will try.
3. Decide what you will each do to make the plan work.
4. Review the progress in one week.

COUPLE EXERCISE 3.1
Improving Your Communication

Once you and your partner have read the chapter on communication, you can explore the uniqueness of your relationship by doing the following exercise. Complete the exercise separately. You can either photocopy the pages or write directly in the book.

List three things you really like about the way your partner communicates.

Partner 1   Partner 2

1. _____   1. _____

2. _____   2. _____

3. _____   3. _____

List three things you would like your partner to change about how he or she communicates.

Partner 1   Partner 2

1. _____   1. _____

2. _____   2. _____

3. _____   3. _____

After you have completed your individual lists, share and discuss them with each other. Talk about the things you agree to work on changing.

REMINDERS FOR IMPROVING
YOUR COMMUNICATION

1. Practice positive communication. When offering criticism as a speaker, balance it with at least one positive comment.

2. Give your full attention to the speaker—turn off your phone, shut off your television, make eye contact with your partner.

3. Focus on the good qualities in each other and praise these often.

4. Take time to listen. Listen to understand, not to judge. After listening, tell your partner what you heard before you share your own ideas. Suspend your emotions until you receive feedback that you have interpreted correctly.

5. Be assertive. Use "I" statements rather than "You" statements. Let your partner know what you want—don't let your needs become a guessing game.

6. Listen with your ears but also with your eyes and other senses.

7. Find the courage to ask questions (rather than making assumptions) until you are clear that you understand your partner.

FOUR

CONFLICT— AN OPPORTUNITY IN DISGUISE

Difficulties are meant to rouse, not discourage.
The human spirit is to grow strong by conflict.

—WILLIAM ELLERY CHANNING

In our national survey of fifty thousand couples, the most significant conflict item discriminating between happy and unhappy couples is whether the partners feel understood when discussing problems. Those in happy relationships are much more likely to feel understood by their partners and to feel able to share feelings and opinions during disagreements. Happy couples are also much more likely to resolve differences and agree on a process of how to address conflict. Finally, partners in happy relationships are much more likely to take their disagreements seriously.

FIGURE 4.1
Strengths of Happy Couples vs. Unhappy Couples
Regarding Conflict Resolution

Relationship Issue	Percentage in Agreement	
	Happy Couples	Unhappy Couples
1. When we discuss problems, my partner understands my opinions and ideas.	78 %	20 %
2. I can share feelings and ideas with my partner during disagreements.	78%	25%
3. We are able to resolve our differences.	58%	12%
4. We have similar ideas about how to settle disagreements.	72%	28%
5. My partner takes our disagreements seriously.	54%	14%

CONFLICT IS MISUNDERSTOOD

Conflict has gotten a bad rap, which we argue is unwarranted. Conflict often gets blamed for the thoughts and behaviors people choose in response to it. This is equivalent to blaming a lousy mood on a rainy day. The reality is not that rain is negative, but it is how a person allows it to define their day. Think of how absurd it would be if a plant could determine rain was negative and it therefore avoided all contact with rain. If this were possible, the plant would simply die. Human "rain" is as necessary as the rain that the natural world needs to survive and to thrive.

It has been said that "conflict is the beginning of consciousness."[1] It jolts us out of our tendency to live our lives on autopilot, forcing us to observe and take notice. Conflict is actually essential for the healthy functioning of a relationship because it allows people to adapt to new situations and to invent new approaches to problems.

What images and feelings come to mind when you think of conflict? Are these images positive or negative? If they are negative, you are likely making these common negative associations with the unpleasant *effects* of conflict, many of which are caused by misunderstanding conflict. As part of this chapter, we hope to reorient you to define conflict as an opportunity within your relationship—an opportunity for observation, deep understanding, creating options, and growth and change.

After all, relationships will surely contain all of life's blessings, pain, joy, surprises, and frustration. Redefining obstacles (conflict) as opportunities can help overcome their negative functions and help you find value in adversity. Adversity is as organic within a relationship as rain is to a plant. At the most minimal and fundamental level, "bad times" provide a contrast and therefore allow us to define "good times." Let's look a little closer at the common conflict problems that married couples report.

COMMON CONFLICT PROBLEMS

Conflict is common and it does not have to damage a relationship. Problems arise when couples do not know how to manage conflict, or when they use it destructively. Our survey identified the top five issues regarding conflict resolution for couples (see Figure 4.2). According to the survey, the biggest issue for most couples is disagreement on who feels responsible for a given problem. In addition, many couples feel their differences never seem to get resolved, and partners will go out of the way to avoid conflict with each other. A majority of couples have different ideas about the best way to solve disagreements and report having serious disputes over trivial matters.

FIGURE 4.2
Top Five Conflict Problems for Couples

Conflict Issue	Percentage of Couples Having Problem*
1. One person ends up feeling responsible for the problem.	80%
2. I go out of my way to avoid conflict with my partner.	78%
3. We have different ideas about the best way to solve disagreements.	77%
4. Some of our differences never seem to get resolved.	77%
5. We sometimes have serious disputes over unimportant issues.	76%

One or both partners indicated this was an issue for them.

EXPECTING THAT CONFLICT WILL NOT EXIST

The idea that conflict should not exist within a marriage is one of the dominating lies that hinders a couple's ability to be happy together. How did this happen? When did we begin to expect that love and joy would occur in a vacuum without pain and adversity? These are in part rhetorical questions, but it is important to reorient ourselves to understand that living is about change—even a life frozen in happiness would eventually feel stagnant.

Real life is a process—like the river, it has movement, life, and depth. This "process" orientation of life helps us understand that since conflict, failure, and disappointment are just part of the process, there is no reason to expend energy avoiding something that is simply part of the package. Who decided that disagreement is a negative thing anyway? Perhaps it is just an opinion circulated into the psyche of common culture. It would certainly be countercultural to describe a rainy day as "beautiful," but in reality rain is no less beautiful than a day without clouds.

Conflict is a natural and inevitable aspect of human relationships. People in a relationship are going to have differences, and relations will not always be harmonious. As partners become closer, their differences in gender, background, and personality will lead to differences of opinion, causing conflict at times. However, the fact that conflict exists in intimate relationships does not necessarily mean that love is absent. In fact, more intimate relationships will often have more conflict. If handled in a healthy way, that conflict will strengthen the relational bond, but if handled wrong, it can break down the relationship.

AVOIDING CONFLICT

A majority of couples in our survey (78 percent) report they go out of their way to avoid conflict with their partner. Couples who ignore problems in hopes they will disappear find the opposite will happen. This always reminds me of a story I (Amy) used to read to my son when he was a little boy. In the story, a young boy notices a small dragon in his home. He repeatedly tells his mother about the dragon, but each time his mother only responds, "There is no such thing as a dragon!" The dragon grows larger as mother and boy continue to ignore the dragon. Finally, the dragon becomes so large that its head, legs, and tail are sticking out of windows and doors. Immediately after the mother and boy acknowledge the dragon, it shrinks down to its original size. The story concludes when the mother and boy wonder, "Why did he have to get so big?" The boy says, "Maybe he just wanted to be noticed."[2]

This provides a good analogy for relational problems. They exist for a reason—they contain a message, a lesson—and they want to be noticed. If the problem is not acknowledged, like the dragon it will continue to fester and grow, eventually leading to feelings of bitterness that cause distance. Every time we ignore a problem in order to avoid conflict, we take a small step away from our partners.

Just as with any physical illness or mechanical breakdown, the sooner you treat a problem, the easier it will be to cure or fix. For example, if you suddenly developed an acute pain in your chest, you would not ignore it because it might be a symptom of a serious illness. The pain is a warning sign, a piece of important information. The same is true in relationships. Feelings of hurt, anger, or sadness are important cues and provide worthy information. It is important not to ignore warning signs telling you that your relationship needs some attention. Problems rarely go away on their own with time, and they often get worse.

ATTACKING THE PERSON, RATHER THAN THE PROBLEM

Another common obstacle to resolving conflict is when partners focus their criticism on the other person rather than on the problem. The other person will almost instinctively become defensive in an attempt to protect herself and to justify her position. Attacking the other person generates hostility rather than resolution.

Blaming is a form of attacking your partner. Blamers spend a lot of time and energy trying to change other people. They essentially try to hold others responsible for their own feelings and see others, rather than themselves, as the source of the problem. But remember this saying: "When you point a finger at someone, there are three fingers pointing back at yourself." In other words, a problem is almost never the fault of only one person; all people involved contribute in some way to the issue.

Assigning blame can become an ineffective and endless cycle. It's critical to understand that other people do not cause your problems or serve as the source of your unhappiness. And since the only person you can change or control is yourself, you might as well use the energy wasted on blaming your partner to clarify your own thoughts, feelings, and preferences. Ask yourself: "What is the real issue here?" What do I want to change?" "What part of this problem can I influence?" "Do I have the power to change?" By focusing on what you desire from the relationship and how that can be achieved, you harness the power you *do* have instead of forfeiting your power by blaming.

WHEN PROBLEMS BECOME PERENNIAL

Have you ever resolved a problem or issue in your relationship and then weeks, months, or even years later that same old problem returns? If so, you are not alone. In our research, 77 percent of married couples report that they have differences that never seem to get resolved. We also discovered a big incentive to resolve these differences: marital happiness. The ability to resolve differences varies greatly from happily to unhappily married couples (58 percent vs. 12 percent).

Bringing up past hurts in relationships often leads to more anger, pain, and defensiveness. So why are couples so tempted to rehash old issues? In many cases, people just want to be understood at a deep level and know their partner "gets it." It is almost as though we tell ourselves, "If she hurt me before in this way, she could hurt me again." You may feel it is not safe to trust your partner in a particular area until you know he or she understands and cares about the past offense. Unfortunately, the typical response to bringing up an old issue is not to listen with empathy but to fuss and complain about the same old song and dance coming up again. This does nothing to resolve the issue, making it tempting to revisit when a similar situation arises in the future.

A few years back, John had one too many drinks at the Thanksgiving celebration hosted by his parents. After the meal as John was watching the game with his brothers and uncles, he began to make crude and offensive remarks about his and Sandy's personal relationship. Sandy could not believe he would say things like that in front of her in-laws, and she was very hurt, embarrassed, and angry. Since that time, she brought the issue up on several occasions, usually when they were going to attend another party or gathering. John would quickly make excuses and downplay his past behavior. He even said he was sorry. To Sandy, however, his "sorry" sounded more like "I wish you'd get over it." She never really believed John understood how betrayed she felt by his remarks, and she still didn't trust that he wouldn't make the same mistake again while drinking with friends or family.

Unfortunately, issues like John and Sandy's are all too common. In looking at the list of strengths of happy couples, it is no coincidence that the majority of satisfied couples feel their partner understands their opinions and ideas, and they are able to resolve their differences. Unhappy couples rarely do either well. Recurring issues from the past should be a signal that the offended individual does not feel understood or listened to. Very often, the best way to put old issues to rest is to use active listening skills that focus on the feelings behind as well as the content of the message.

CONFLICT AND ANGER

> "Speak when you are angry—and you'll make the best speech you'll ever regret."
>
> DR. LAURENCE J. PETERS

Just as perceptions about conflict get in the way of empowering your relationship, views on anger also can inhibit intimacy. Keep in mind that anger is a normal and healthy human emotion. Anger is a natural adaptive response to threats, signaling to us when we are getting into physically and emotionally unsafe situations. So first of all, learn to become conscious of when you feel angry. Anger is usually a symptom of some issue within the relationship that needs to be addressed and possibly changed.

Once you notice the anger, you must be careful and deliberate in channeling it constructively. There is a popular saying, "Anger is one letter short of danger." This is because there are several damaging ways in which anger is handled. One is suppression. When anger is not allowed to be expressed, but just pushed inside and ignored, it becomes dangerous to ourselves and to our relationship. Suppressing anger toward your partner only causes bitterness and resentment. You may put on a happy face temporarily, but your relationship will suffer eventually. Some people repress anger for a time but then reach a threshold and explode in unpredictable rages.

Holding on to anger can also turn inward, resulting in personal anxiety, depression, addiction, and physical illness. These are such common ailments partly because anger is regarded as a socially negative emotion. We are taught that anger is not OK, while anxiety and depression are more socially acceptable. Unexpressed anger can also manifest itself in a demeanor that is perpetually cynical, sarcastic, or critical. Not surprisingly, individuals who express anger in these passive-aggressive ways often do not have very happy relationships.

Expressing anger can be done constructively, but it can also be done in ways that destroy relationships. Destructive expressions of anger blame, shame, or attack the other person, alienating her from you and undermining your credibility.

A healthy expression of anger is non-judgmental, direct, and straightforward. It makes clear our needs without hurting the other person. It reflects an understanding that others do not cause our feelings or behaviors. Anger is something we need to *respond* to, not *react* to. Doing so enhances communication and personal growth, and it demonstrates being true to one's feelings, which helps elicit trust from others.

IMPROVING YOUR ABILITY TO RESOLVE CONFLICT

The following are ways to improve your conflict resolution skills . . . thereby improving your overall relationship satisfaction.

Embrace Conflict

It may seem strange to begin the discussion on how to improve conflict resolution with the advice of embracing conflict. But attitudinally, we must redefine conflict as a normal and natural aspect of life. Many couples are afraid of the negative emotions associated with addressing their problems. They choose to ignore issues, hoping they will disappear with time. But guess what happens? Like the dragon in the children's book, the problem grows until it gets noticed. In the meantime, the unacknowledged issue may have caused resentment or bitterness in one or both partners. In their extensive couple research, Howard Markman and colleagues identified avoidance as one of the key relationship patterns that is predictive of unhappiness and divorce.[3] A new study published in *Psychosomatic Medicine* found that women who keep silent during arguments were four times more likely to die during the ten-year study parameters than women who spoke their minds. Keeping silent to "keep the peace" is linked to depression, heart disease, and eating disorders.[4] We need to get this clear: avoiding conflict is not good for individuals or for relationships.

Not only is conflict normal, but it is purposeful. There are hidden opportunities inside conflict that can strengthen the marital bond beyond what is possible in solely harmonious exchanges. When conflict is not manifested as anger, competition, or blame, there are opportunities to learn about yourself and your partner. When handled constructively, a deeper bond is created. It takes some work to bring out this potential in conflict, but the rewards are worth the effort. This work involves practicing a few basic skill sets, but one of the most important things you can do is to embrace conflict as an opportunity to learn and strengthen your relationship.

Approaching conflict with this "learning" frame of mind reduces the probability that it will be used in one of two common but ineffective ways: as competition and as a problem to solve. *Conflict as competition* is often exhibited by partners battling to come out ahead. This may serve egos or personal interests in the short-term, but ultimately it diminishes the relationship. If one person feels as if they "won" the argument, then there must be a loser. In relationship if one loses, both lose, because a great partnership must be cooperative venture.

Engaging in *conflict as a problem to be solved* is enticing but can be ineffective. Granted, there will often be underlying issues to resolve, and we will provide a formulaic way to approach these so that extraneous issues will be kept to a minimum. But even so, the underlying meaning behind conflict is easily overlooked with the solution-focused approach. For instance, we see couples arguing about role expectations, and "solving the problem" of who does the laundry may not resolve the underlying issue of an unbalanced sense of justice, respect, and fairness.

Conflict is not an opportunity to win or lose or solve a problem; it is a learning opportunity. Adopting this attitude heightens our curiosity, allowing us to not just be at the mercy of the ups and downs of life but to let them serve us; providing opportunities for our bond to deepen and to flourish. If your partner is angry or upset, it is a sign to you that important feelings have been stirred up and he or she truly cares about the issue at hand. Understanding the strong feelings helps you to learn and connect at a deeper level.

If you find yourself wanting to be "right" about how "wrong" you think your partner is, let go of the urge to correct by concentrating on *connecting*. Start by listening carefully to how he came to feel the way he does. Most of the time by doing this you will be able to honestly say, "You're right. I understand when you explain it from your perspective. Now this is my point of view . . ." One of the tenets of psychotherapy is that people need to feel validated and accepted *as they are* before they are willing and able to change. Validating your partner's perspective does not mean you have to *agree*; it only means you can understand. And when someone feels understood they put less effort into defining and defending their position and are open to hearing others' positions as well.

Know Your Dance of Conflict

In working with hundreds of couples in marital therapy, we've noticed a cycle that emerges into a predictable "dance of conflict" fueled by emotional attacks and defensive reactions. For most couples, their dance is predictable, even when the topic of the conflict changes.

It starts when "buttons are pushed" at an emotional level. Typical buttons for men include feelings of inadequacy and disrespect. When men hear messages that sound like "you're a failure," "you don't measure up," or "I don't respect who you are or what you do," it hits them at a core level that feels very threatening and seems to demand a defense of their self-worth.

> "An argument is always about what has been made more important than the relationship."
>
> HUGH PRATHNER

Typical buttons for women include messages and feelings around value, care, and love. When women see behavior or hear messages that translate as "I don't care about you," "you're worthless," or "you're unlovable," they are shaken at a self-worth level that demands their own defense. Whether or not an individual is consciously aware of her feelings, these are very scary messages. When humans feel attacked, even at these emotional levels, there is typically an underlying feeling of fear that generates a physiological response of fight or flight.

Like the emotional buttons in the dance of conflict, defensive fight-or-flight responses are also somewhat predictable. Fight responses include escalating behaviors such as criticism, yelling, aggression, and pursuit of the other person. These responses are intended to quiet the perceived threat by overcoming and subduing it. Flight responses include behaviors that help one retreat, distract, soothe, or distance themselves. The silent treatment, avoidance, or leaving the scene altogether are obvious flight responses. But other strategies that distract and sooth a hurting individual include addictions that provide an escape or rush (such as substance abuse, gambling, compulsive shopping, or pornography). Unfortunately, the very defensive behaviors that couples tend to adopt often push the emotional buttons of their partners, thereby fueling the cycle all over again.

> It seemed every time the credit card statement came, Will and Ruth had another argument that followed their typical script. It was their goal to pay off the credit cards and get out from under the burden of high interest rates. But in reviewing their bill, Will would notice new shopping purchases that Ruth had made without his knowledge. He was immediately angry and would go to her, criticizing and complaining about her judgment and lack of self-control. She would try to justify her purchases, but on some level the underlying message in Will's attack communicated that he cared more about their bills than her. In her defense, she would sometimes criticize him, stating that if he earned more, like all the other men in his family, this would not even be an issue. At that point, Will would shut down and pull away in response to feeling like a failure as a provider. The more he pulled away, the more Ruth felt unloved. She would often soothe these feelings through the distraction and excitement of shopping. It was a predictable and viscous cycle in their dance of conflict.

Have the Strength to Be Vulnerable

Fear and vulnerability are closely interrelated to conflict. Let's face it: we are all vulnerable as human beings. We get sad; we become ill; we eventually die. We are afraid of our vulnerability, and this fear can lead to conflict. Ironically, the only way to successfully navigate the conflict is to face these vulnerabilities. We can elect not to, and many do. Many people hate conflict and vulnerability so much that they end up asking much less from their relationships than they should. Technology is not much help: we can now hide our isolation beneath the guise of connection in e-mail, chat rooms, and text messages. But to be truly connected in the world and in our relationships, we must enter the zone of engagement by being vulnerable.

> "We are healed of suffering only by expressing it to the full."
>
> MARCEL PROUST

Attempting to avoid your vulnerability is the very thing that causes the pain or ailments that stem from not allowing yourself to feel your vulnerabilities. Suppressed grief, sadness, and rage easily devolve into depression, anxiety, and addiction. Concealed fear often turns into panic disorders, phobias, prejudice, or even violence. Grief, fear, and despair are primary emotions, as fundamental to human existence as love, awe, joy, and hope. Denying or numbing these emotions does nothing to reduce the suffering they engender; unexpressed, they only may become hidden and more complicated to decipher. Remember: these emotions offer themselves as a means of individual and relational transformation and healing. They are important sources of information. They also connect us to others, helping us to develop empathy and compassion.

Honor all your emotions by allowing them to be expressed in the safety of your relationship. You will find that you will be released into the joy of knowing that you can live with and use all of your emotions to develop empathy, nurturance, and care for others. As psychotherapist Miriam Greenspan expresses so wisely:

> We learn to accept suffering and vulnerability as a normal part of life, and how to use our suffering for the good. Because we are vulnerable, life hurts. We are not here to be free of pain. We are here to have our hearts broken by life, and to transform our pain to love.[5]

True intimacy is possible and difficult precisely because it requires vulnerability. To let your partner know your needs and fears is scary for some people. It means giving someone access to deeper parts of yourself.

Do Not Stockpile Grievances

Stockpiling is temporarily suppressing negative emotions that come up in your relationship. Initially this is often done as a way to overlook little annoyances and to avoid conflict, but the problem is they often are not truly overlooked but cataloged. Stockpiling leads to major blowups over what looks like one little grievance, but it is actually that one plus ten prior unacknowledged grievances. This phenomenon is a great example of what we hope you have noticed to be a major theme of this book. That is, the only way to move beyond something is to go through it. All the things we do to avoid what we think will be unpleasant experiences—from dismissing them to trivializing them to completely ignoring them—are futile.

As human beings, we often make the mistake of ignoring our feelings, but to do so is to avoid truth, which can never be done without consequence. The consequence of not addressing the little grievances in your relationship as they come about is that they will grow in power. To release their power and let them fade into the past, express them as they occur. The following are some simple ground rules to keep in mind so these grievances do not become hurtful to the receiver.

Studies find it is not whether or not a couple fights that predicts divorce, but *how* they fight. For example, if one person bears all responsibility or the fight turns into a character assault, one or both people will end up feeling lousy or resentful. These ground rules keep fighting fair and respectful:

- **Focus on the behavior, not the person.** People universally will defend themselves when they feel attacked. They are less likely to become defensive, and therefore more likely to listen, when you present behavior-focused feedback.

- **Say it respectfully.** Disrespectful words block communication and create wounds. Hurtful words are long-remembered and make one less willing to share or be vulnerable.

- **Be specific.** Do not generalize; avoid words such as "always" or "never." Acknowledge specific behaviors and how they affect you.

- **Remember good communication skills.** Make use of the communication skills discussed in chapter 3: maintain eye contact, use "I" statements, identify feelings, and use active listening.

- **Use humor.** Humor is great for breaking down negative emotions. Be careful to use humor appropriately, though. An easy way to show respect in using humor is to allow yourself to be the target of the joke.

- **Take your partner seriously.** While you may use humor with discretion, it is imperative that you take your partner seriously and demonstrate this with respect.

- **Deal with the present.** The past is the past and needs to be left there. Limit yourself to only discussing relevant, present issues.

- **Stay calm.** It is more likely that your partner will consider your viewpoint when you speak calmly.

- **Keep your arguments private.** Resist the urge to discuss your private conflicts with friends or family. You will eventually work the problem out or make up, but your friends or family members may continue to carry anger or resentment toward your partner.

- **If you cannot agree** . . . at least respect your partner's feelings and opinions.

CONSTRUCTIVE CONFLICT

By now you recognize that "constructive conflict" is *not* an oxymoron. Conflict can serve your relationship by deepening your connection and level of intimacy. The basic idea is to *understand* differences, so you can be a protagonist in your relationship and have an active role in its outcome. This process is two-fold: you must first know how you currently deal with conflict and then determine how you would like to handle it in the future.

> "I would not waste my life in friction when it could be turned into momentum."
>
> FRANCES WILLARD

The Couple Checkup section on conflict resolution will give you information on how you currently handle conflict. The results you have as a couple, as well as the national survey results on happy and unhappy couples, should serve as a guide to where you would like to be in terms of conflict resolution.

During times of conflict, does your partner understand you? If so, it is likely that you both are using constructive conflict-resolution skills. If not, you may have to change your approach, especially if you want to be among happily married couples. Happily married couples overwhelmingly report feeling that their opinions and ideas are understood when they are discussing problems (87 percent vs. 19 percent). The good news is that these modes of communication can be learned and refined.

Many components of conflict resolution allow for different approaches, and the approaches used will dramatically affect the outcome and the feelings of the partners involved. Some approaches are constructive while others are destructive. Let's examine both.

When using destructive approaches to conflict resolution, a person brings up old issues. In constructive conflict resolution, the focus is on the relevant and current issues.

When partners argue destructively, they express only negative feelings; in constructive conflict resolution, they share both positive and negative feelings.

Destructive quarrelers share only select information with each other as they try to hold the other partner responsible. Constructive conflict resolution does not point fingers of blame but shares the facts of the situation, even if they do not always support an individual's contention. Further, the reality that both partners contribute to the problem is emphasized.

Destructive conflict resolution resists change, while constructive approaches encourage change in order to develop new ways of handling problems.

And, perhaps most noteworthy, the level of emotional closeness decreases when couples engage in destructive conflict resolution; the result of constructive conflict resolution is often increased intimacy and trust in the relationship.

Figure 4.3 compares the various components of constructive and destructive approaches to conflict resolution, as well as the outcome of each. Because the approach you use to resolve conflict will affect the outcome, the more constructive your approach, the greater the possibility of success.

FIGURE 4.3

Constructive and Destructive Approaches to Conflict Resolution

Area of Concern	Constructive Approach	Destructive Approach
Issues	Raises and clarifies current issues	Brings up old issues
Feelings	Expresses both positive and negative feelings	Expresses only negative feelings
Information	Gives complete and honest information	Offers only select information
Focus	Concentrates on the issue rather than the person	Concentrates on the person rather than the issue
Blame	Accepts mutual blame	Blames the other person for the problem
Perception	Focuses on similarities	Focuses on differences
Change	Facilitates change to prevent stagnation	Minimizes change, increasing conflict
Outcome	Recognizes both must win or both lose	A loss for the relationship
Intimacy	Increases intimacy by resolving conflict	Decreases intimacy by escalating conflict
Attitude	Builds trust	Creates suspicion

TEN STEPS FOR RESOLVING COUPLE CONFLICT

One of the secrets of using conflict to strengthen your relationship is adopting the attitude and expectation that conflict is normal. We have discussed how a healthy dose of conflict is often an opportunity in disguise. But there will certainly be times in your marriage when conflict involves the need to make a

> "When patterns are broken, new worlds emerge."
>
> TULI KUPFERBERG

decision. For these situations, this ten-step model is a formulaic way to work through the issue step by step with your partner. These ten steps help you to focus on the problem, not on the emotions that often accompany problems. They will also keep you from deviating from the issue at hand, which is so easy to do. When you have ongoing issues or decisions that need to be made, use this ten-step approach to deal with them.

The following is an explanation of each step, along with an example of how a married couple, Gary and Melissa, used the ten-step procedure to work through an issue. In the exercise at the end of the chapter, you can use these ten steps to work through one of your own issues. You will probably find that this formula, by forcing you to stay centered, on task, and brainstorm new ideas, will break open old, unresolved issues. So focus on one issue at a time, allowing yourselves at least thirty minutes to complete the exercise. Then try the solution for one week.

1. **Set a time and place for discussion.** Gary and Melissa set aside thirty minutes on Saturday afternoon at two o'clock to share and discuss, focusing on one specific issue.

2. **Define the problem or issue of disagreement.** The issue they have chosen is a complaint of Gary's, and it has caused tension in their relationship several times before. Gary is upset because he feels Melissa makes decisions without asking his opinion. He feels disrespected.

3. **Talk about how each of you contributes to the problem.** Melissa admits to making plans without asking for Gary's input. Gary concedes that he is often indecisive and that Melissa is a better decision maker. Still, Gary often feels as if he has little control over how they spend time as a couple.

4. **List unsuccessful past attempts to resolve the issue.** After this first became an issue, Melissa began asking Gary about upcoming

"potential" dinner dates or family events after she had already told the other party they would attend. If Gary was uninterested or unable to go, this caused problems to both their relationship and in cancelling plans to which Melissa had already committed.

5. **Brainstorm ten new ways to resolve the conflict.** For instance, Melissa will not make major decisions without consulting Gary. Gary will try to be more assertive in expressing his preferences. They will not make rush decisions. Each night after dinner, Melissa and Gary will discuss upcoming plans. They will check and recheck with each other about plans. Neither Melissa nor Gary will make any new plans for the next week. Gary will make all the plans for a week. Melissa will adopt a standard response to invitations such as, "Let me check my and Gary's calendars and get back to you."

6. **Discuss and evaluate these possible solutions.** Melissa and Gary talk about each solution and share with each other what they like and dislike about each one.

7. **Agree on one solution to try.** Melissa and Gary decide to start discussing upcoming plans with each other every night after dinner.

8. **Agree on how each of you will work toward this solution.** Melissa agrees to not make any plans without consulting Gary, and Gary agrees to practice being assertive by asking about plans at dinner.

9. **Set up another meeting to discuss your progress.** Melissa and Gary decide to meet again next Saturday at two o'clock to discuss how they feel the plan is working.

10. **Reward each other as you each contribute toward the solution.** Melissa and Gary plan to treat themselves to dinner at their favorite restaurant as a reward for their efforts toward resolving this issue.

CHECK-IN PROCESS

Where are you *now*? (Identify and discuss your results.)

1. Review the Couple Checkup *individual* results. How satisfied were each of you in this area?

_____

_____

2. Review the Couple Checkup *couple* results. Was conflict resolution a strength or growth area?

_____

_____

3. Discuss your agreement items (your strengths).

_____

_____

Where would you like to be? (Discuss issues.)

1. Review the discussion items in your Couple Checkup report.
2. Choose one issue you both want to resolve.
3. Share how you each feel about the issue.

How do you get there? (Develop your action plan.)

1. Brainstorm a list of ways to handle your conflict resolution problems.
2. Agree on one solution you will try.
3. Decide what you will each do to make the plan work.
4. Review the progress in one week.

COUPLE EXERCISE 4.1
Ten-Step Procedure for Resolving Conflict

Use this ten-step model when there is a frequent problem you have not been able to resolve. Try it with your partner now. Start with a minor ongoing issue in your relationship.

In step five, brainstorm at least ten new ways to resolve the issue. Do not judge ideas based on whether they are feasible. Simply come up with as many ideas as possible, even if they may seem far-fetched. Brainstorming in this way will allow you to get beyond what you have done in the past that has not worked.

1. Set a time and place for discussion. Be specific.

   _____

2. Define the problem or issue of disagreement.

   _____

   _____

3. Talk about how each of you contributes to the problem.

   _____

   _____

   _____

4. List unsuccessful past attempts to resolve the issue.

   _____

   _____

   _____

5. Brainstorm ten new ways to resolve the conflict.

   _____   _____

   _____   _____

   _____   _____

   _____   _____

   _____   _____

6. Discuss and evaluate these possible solutions.

_____

_____

_____

_____

7. Agree on one solution to try.

_____

8. Agree on how each of you will work toward this solution.

_____

_____

_____

_____

9. Set up another meeting to discuss your progress.

_____

10. Reward each other as you each contribute toward the solution.

_____

_____

_____

REMINDERS FOR IMPROVING YOUR ABILITY TO RESOLVE CONFLICT

1. View conflict as a normal and healthy part of a close relationship.

2. Never negotiate in moments of anger. Take some time to compose yourself so that you will be able to rationally discuss the issue.

3. When negotiating, do not bring up past issues. Stay in the present. It is the only place where things are really happening.

4. Do not blame each other, but focus on the problem. Remember that everyone involved contributes in some way.

5. Deal directly with issues as they arise. If an issue keeps coming up, use the ten-step model to work through it.

6. Validate. Allow your spouse to have and express his or her experience. Have a discussion about the problem, without highlighting the fact that one of you may agree and the other may disagree.

7. Do not stockpile. Storing up hurt feelings and grievances is counterproductive. Let your partner know about the things that bother you as they occur.

8. Consider yourselves allies rather than adversaries in problem solving.

9. Be honest. Arguments quickly turn ugly when a partner does not feel they are being told the whole truth.

10. Create a win-win solution.

FIVE

FINANCES— MORE THAN MONEY

To some people, money means power; to others, love.
For some, the topic is boorish, in bad taste. For others,
it's more private than sex. Add family dynamics to the
mix, and for many you have the subject from hell.

—KAREN S. PETERSON

In the throes of new love, "What's mine is yours" is as easy a sentiment as it is romantic. Couples are rarely able to uphold this ease of attitude about finances because money represents much more than just money. There are underlying psychological issues in how we relate to money and how money plays out in our relationship. Money operates metaphorically in our lives representing things such as security, nurturance, trust, opportunity, and the relationship between dependence and independence. Little wonder then, money is a major cause of conflict and a multilayered problem for couples.

THE REAL COST OF MONEY

If you sometimes feel as though financial issues dominate your life, you are not alone. It is estimated that we spend up to 80 percent of our waking hours earning money, spending money, or thinking about money. A survey conducted by American Express Financial Advisors revealed that 66 percent of

> ## "Money often costs too much."
>
> RALPH WALDO
> EMERSON

Americans spend more time thinking about money and careers than they do about sex, health, or relationships.

What's more, financial issues are the most common source of stress for couples and families. Historically, economics was an important reason *for* marriage, whereas today finances are a common contributor to divorce. Money problems are now second only to infidelity as a cause of divorce.[1] In a study that examined couples' problems as reported to marital therapists, 43 percent of couples reported that money management was a frequent problem in their marriage.[2]

MORE . . . IS IT BETTER?

As a nation, America has had an enormously productive economy, affording us an abundance of luxuries and material goods. Today, even lower-class individuals often have access to things such as heat and air conditioning, which were considered luxuries even to royalty years ago. Compared to the 1950s, people in the U.S. in 1991 owned twice as many cars and drove two and a half times as much every year.

In fact, the word *more* accurately describes much of how our lifestyles and possessions have changed over time: we drive more vehicles, spend more time at work, watch more television, spend more time shopping, produce more garbage, consume more fossil fuels, spend more money, and have more debt than any generation in history. There is a clear upward trend in our consumption habits—everything from the size of the homes we live in to the amount of food we waste.[3] Yet, it seems as though our ever-rising standard of living has not resulted in a higher quality of life.

QUANTITY DOES NOT EQUAL QUALITY

A couple we saw in counseling quite innocuously fell into the allure of having more, only to find themselves feeling impoverished by their new lifestyle:

Phil was a successful businessman, and his income provided enough for Debbie to be at home with their two daughters, ages two and five. This made the decision to leave her job as a mechanical engineer easier for Debbie. She was an incredible mom and loved the freedom of spending time with their girls every day for five years.

Unexpectedly, Debbie was approached to work part-time in a new start-up company. After deliberating over the offer, Phil and Debbie decided it was a great opportunity for her to get in on the "ground floor" of a promising new venture. Plus, it was only part-time, and she'd still have plenty of time at home with the girls. With the increased income, Phil pushed the idea of buying a much larger and much more expensive home.

It was not long before the start-up company Debbie worked for was purchased by a larger company. The new company said they wanted Debbie full-time and offered her a promotion and a raise she could not refuse. Her new position required long hours and occasional out-of-town travel, but she enjoyed the challenge. Debbie and Phil hired a live-in nanny to take care of the girls. Between the new house and the expense of a full-time nanny, they could no longer afford their lifestyle unless Debbie continued working full-time.

Phil and Debbie came to couple counseling three years after the purchase of their new home. They were experiencing significant marital and personal stress. While they were both quite fulfilled with their careers, the demands left little time and energy for themselves or their daughters. Debbie explained, "I feel caught in a bind. I love my career, but I feel like I am missing out on our daughter's childhood. Sometimes I think about buying a cheaper home so I can work part-time again, but then I feel guilty about uprooting our children from this community. Our older daughter is in third grade at the neighborhood school and our five-year-old's best friend lives next door."

As we explored this couple's financial picture, it became clear they had fallen victim to what sociologists call an "upscaling" of desires and expectations.

Phil and Debbie were bringing home a combined income of $220,000 annually. The bigger mortgage was not the only demand on the $90,000 Debbie brought home from her job. It turns out they replaced a lot of their furniture when they moved, as well as bought new cars. Phil admits the pressure to replace their existing cars was due to the social statements he perceived the new cars to make. He says, "Our home is in a pretty affluent neighborhood. Everyone drives new or newer cars. Our old cars just didn't fit in."

Debbie's feeling of being in a bind was well justified. Their new home, furniture, and cars have done little to enhance their lives yet have caused a financial squeeze which steals time away from their family. For Phil and Debbie, saying yes to these new possessions caused them indirectly to say no to their relationship and their children.

Phil and Debbie represent a lot of families today. Despite having more wealth and more material possessions, the percentage of Americans who feel significantly well-off has decreased. Between the years 1970 and 1990 there has been a staggering 51 percent decrease in the quality of life in the U.S. as measured by the index of Social Health. The flip side of doing "more" (e.g., more work), is that other activities need to decrease in order to accommodate the time to do more.

Unfortunately, the activities we eliminate are often those that add quality and dimension to our relationships. For example, the average American spends twenty-eight hours per week watching television, six hours per week shopping, but only forty minutes per week playing with their children. The endless pursuit of more income to pay for bigger mortgages or to buy more stuff we do not need leaves insufficient time and energy to enjoy family, friends, and outside interests. How can we live a quality life in an endless pursuit of more?

In their book *Psychology and Consumer Culture*, Tim Kasser and Allen Kanner posit that cultures of overabundance and greed leave people disconnected between their wants and their needs. The authors make the statement that "materialism appears to be toxic to subjective *wellbeing*" and is damaging to relationships.[4] "Materialism" refers to a preoccupation with money and material goods. It often manifests itself as the purchasing of new goods and services with little attention to their true need, durability, product origin, or the environmental toll in the manufacturing and disposal of these items. Material goods have no intrinsic value, so are promoted relentlessly by corporations who profit from the sale of these items. Problems with mindless and excessive consumerism are far-reaching and have been documented to negatively affect society, the environment, and the economy, but this discussion will be limited to how consumerism interferes with healthy families, individuals, and marriages.

EXPERIENCING LACK IN A CULTURE OF ABUNDANCE

Consumerism interferes with interpersonal relationships by replacing the normal commonsense desire for an adequate supply of life's necessities—community life, a stable family, and healthy relationships—with an ongoing and insatiable quest for things. We can assume it is this quest for things that has led to a substantial increase in consumer debt and bankruptcies. Many studies have found a link between financial problems and marital dissatisfaction and divorce.[5] But even in marriages and families without debt or financial strain, using money as a basis for success and happiness is sure to disappoint.

> "Happiness is not in the mere possession of money; it lies in the joy of achievement, in the thrill of creative effort."
>
> FRANKLIN DELANO ROOSEVELT

Despite astounding economic growth and overall increase in material possessions and wealth, Americans report feeling significantly less well-off than they did twenty-two years ago. The very livelihood of many companies depends on consumers buying into the lie that their product will make us happy, when research clearly shows that family and significant relationships, not material possessions or being wealthy, are what makes people happy.[6] Research also shows that materialistic people tend to have poor personal relationships.[7]

So our fixation on wealth and material objects becomes a self-perpetuating cycle. In a misguided attempt to find value or meaning in life, we buy products instead of relating better to people. Manufacturers produce new things for us to purchase, and we work more to buy or accumulate more debt to pay for these things. We attach less meaning to human relationships and become increasingly self-centered and preoccupied with material goods. And then we create a new generation of people who do the exact same thing.

Not many marriages seem to be immune to problems or potential problems centering on money. No matter how much money families have, they always seem to need more. Family therapists point out, however, that many of these arguments are not really about money. Arguments about money may reflect an inability to develop an open and well-organized couple or family system. These arguments also may represent conflict over power and control in the couple relationship, differing styles of spending and saving, or different visions of what money can and cannot do, as well as the myriad of personal feelings that money invokes for each individual.

COMMON MONEY-RELATED PROBLEMS

> "Home life ceases to be free and beautiful as soon as it is founded on borrowing and debt."
>
> HENRIK IBSEN
> (1828–1906)

Couples have trouble dealing with money issues for a number of reasons, as our national survey of fifty thousand married couples reveals (see Figure 5.1). A majority of problems occurs when one partner thinks the other should be more careful about spending. Although the current trend to marry later in life benefits these couples on many levels, they may have more adjusting to do when it comes to merging partners' finances. Individuals who marry later are accustomed to making money decisions without having to consult another person.

84

FIGURE 5.1
Top Five Financial Problems for Couples

Financial Issue	Percentage of Couples Having Problem*
1. I wish my partner was more careful in spending money.	72%
2. We have trouble saving money.	71%
3. We have problems deciding what is important to purchase.	63%
4. Major debts are a problem for us.	56%
5. Credit card use has been a problem for us.	52%

One or both partners indicated this was an issue for them.

COMMON FINANCIAL STRUGGLES FOR MARRIED COUPLES

Let's look briefly into some of the common financial problems in marriage.

Spender vs. Saver

Spenders and savers are the two classic money personalities. The top two financial issues for a majority of married couples in our national survey related to spending and saving. Not surprisingly, saving and spending problems are common because individuals often have different personal styles of spending and saving. Most

> "Money talks—
> unfortunately
> mine only knows
> how to say
> 'Goodbye.'"
>
> AS SEEN ON
> BUMPER STICKER

partners do not find out until after marriage how different their spending and saving styles really are. The greater the difference in styles, the greater the potential for conflict over money.

To better understand the different styles, it helps to visualize a continuum of saving and spending. On one end of the continuum are people who seem to throw money away. These spenders love to spend money on themselves and on others. They may have personality types that identify more with spenders: spontaneous, extroverted, and less organized. On the other end of the continuum are people who compulsively save money. These savers may feel anxious about spending money or worry that there won't be enough. The classic saver personality type is conservative and very organized.

While many people are somewhere in the middle of the continuum and are able to successfully balance their impulses to spend money with their need to save and budget, others lean toward being either a spender or a saver. It is these differences in tendencies that can cause trouble or lead to disagreements with each other.

Heather likes to joke that she is "good for the economy: the money comes in, and it goes right back out." This is my (Peter's) wife's way of saying that she is more of a spender than a saver. While neither of us is extreme, I'm certainly closer to the other end of the continuum. We were newlyweds preparing for our first Christmas together as a married couple when this difference became very clear. As we were out shopping, Heather came across some beautiful hand-made Christmas stockings. She immediately expressed an interest in purchasing them, despite the seventy-five-dollar price tag. The idea of spending that much on decorations was inconceivable to me at the time. I was a graduate student, and Heather was teaching at a small private school. This type of purchase would eat up a large part of our small budget. This exchange led to our first major conflict. In the months that followed, we realized that making financial decisions was the most difficult area in our marriage and the thing that most often led to conflict. She is more of a spender, and I am more of a saver.

OVERUSE OF CREDIT AND CREDIT CARDS

Overspending is another common money problem, one that often is caused by buying on credit. Although buying on credit is very convenient, credit cards make it easy to overspend and get into debt. Once in the hole, it is a long climb out. The high interest rates on credit card balances (often double—or more—the rate on bank loans) can make it difficult for many people to pay back more than just the interest and finance charges on their debt. Paying the minimum fee each month may seem easier than paying cash for purchases, but you ultimately end up paying much more for that purchase because of the accumulating interest rates.

> "Modern man drives a mortgaged car over a bond-financed highway on credit card gas."
>
> EARL WILSON

The average American has nine credit cards and twenty-seven thousand dollars in credit card debt.[8] You must realize that by carrying a balance on your credit card, you end up paying two, three, or even four or more times the sticker price for your purchases. Do not let the convenience of a credit card break your financial lives.

Blake and Ashley are a young married couple who purchased their first home three years ago. Although they both work, they have not yet added a savings account into their budget. So when their washing machine broke, they went out without much hesitation and bought a new one. With the thought that their new machine would last a long time, they purchased a decent, front-loading, energy-efficient model for $649. After taxes, it cost them $700, all of which they put on their credit card. If they were to make the minimum payment of $20 per month on their credit card at the rate of 19.8 percent interest, it will take them nearly five years until the washing machine is paid for. Worst of all, they will have ended up paying $1,090, and this is only including the interest, not finance charges or additional fees that credit card companies often tack on.

So what were their other options? Ideally, they would have begun saving a percentage of their earnings from the time they bought their home in anticipation of these events. If they had started putting just twenty dollars a month, for example, into a home savings account, they would have had the money to pay for the machine up front. But they didn't, so the credit card was the only option they had, right? Actually not. By simply budgeting thirty dollars per month into a savings account, instead of buying the washing machine on credit, Blake and Ashley would have the cash to pay for the machine in only fourteen months' time. In the meantime, they could wash their clothes at a Laundromat (or perhaps use a relative's or friend's machine) once a week. Saving $390 dollars may be well worth a little inconvenience for this couple.

LACK OF SAVINGS OR A SAVING PLAN

"Beware of little expenses, a small leak will sink a great ship."

BENJAMIN FRANKLIN
(1706–1790)

To figure out how you are doing in terms of your savings, figure out your average annual income and then multiply that by the number of years you have been working. Do not worry about being perfectly accurate; simply estimate the total amount of money that you have earned over your lifetime. Now, look at your savings account balance. If you are like most people, the amount you have saved is probably a very small percentage of the money that has passed through your hands. After taxes and monthly bills, most families have very little money left over to save or invest.

Some people are simply unaware of the benefits of saving. Others make the mistake of thinking of saving as merely another demand on their paycheck. Fortunately, it does not take a lot of money to benefit from compounded interest. And savings are important for creating financial security and being prepared for financial crises such as illness, job loss, pregnancy, or accidents. Figure 5.2 shows how compounding interest allows a little bit of money to grow to substantial sums. Time is on your side when it comes to saving for the future.

FIGURE 5.2
If You Save $1 a Day
($1 per day for 30 days = $30 per month)

Years Saved	5 Percent Interest	10 Percent Interest
10	$4,677	$6,195
20	$12,381	$22,968
30	$25,071	$68,379
40	$45,969	$191,301
50	$80,391	$524,061
60	$137,085	$1,424,856
70	$230,460	$3,863,340

WHAT DOES MONEY MEAN TO YOU?

Money is not simply the paper, coin, or plastic used to buy things. Money is also a mechanism of social exchange. It can be a source of status, security, enjoyment, or control. If partners have incompatible attitudes about money, purchases are more likely to cause conflict between them. Miriam Arond and Samuel Pauker have identified four common orientations toward money:

1. **Money as status.** A person with a status orientation toward money is interested in money as power—as a means of keeping ahead of his peers.

2. **Money as security.** A person with a security orientation is conservative in spending and focuses on saving.

3. Money as enjoyment. A person with an enjoyment orientation gets satisfaction from spending, both on others and on herself.

4. Money as control. A person with a control orientation sees money as a way of maintaining control over his life and independence from a partner or other family members.[9]

It is possible for a person to have more than one orientation, but not two conflicting approaches—for example, enjoyment and security. A questionnaire for assessing your money orientation is provided in Couple Exercise 5.1 at the end of this chapter.

FINANCIAL STRENGTHS OF HAPPY COUPLES

In general, even happy couples disagree more about finances than any other topic. However, our national survey revealed clear differences between happy and unhappy couples regarding money issues (see Figure 5.3). Happy couples agree on how to handle money significantly more than unhappy couples do. They also have fewer concerns about debts and the proper amount to save. Clearly, one way to improve your couple relationship is to discuss and come to a place of agreement on relevant financial matters.

FIGURE 5.3
Strengths of Happy Couples Versus Unhappy Couples
Regarding Finances

Financial Issue	Percentage in Agreement	
	Happy Couples	Unhappy Couples
1. We agree on how to spend money.	85%	43%
2. I am satisfied with our decision to save.	67%	29%

3. Major debts are not a problem for us.	**69%**	**35%**
4. My partner does not try to control our finances.	**74%**	**43%**
5. Credit cards are not a problem for us.	**69%**	**42%**

IMPROVING YOUR FINANCIAL RELATIONSHIP

The following are ways to improve your relationship to finances . . . thereby improving your relationship with your partner.

Recognize the Limitations of Money

Many problems people have with money may be socially induced. Unfortunately, in our culture the standard definition of *success* is financial wealth. A statement such as "he is very successful" generally refers to the acquisition of money, not the quality of a life. As a result, many people are engaged in an endless endeavor to accumulate more money, falsely assuming that money will bring them happiness or fulfillment. These people can easily miss all the joys of the present moment, because their sights are set on a future that is not even guaranteed to exist.

"The real measure of a man's wealth is how much he'd be worth if he lost all his money."

J. H. JOWETT

"Success" as a social construct of financial earnings may be losing momentum. A poll from the AARP (American Association of Retired Persons) shows the most important factors defining success in life include having a good marriage, having a good relationship with one's children, helping those in need, having an interesting job, and being well educated. Between 79 and 94 percent of survey respondents considered each of these essential to happiness, while only 27 percent considered earning a lot of money necessary for success.[10]

In the course of creating your financial goals, it is important to realistically discern what money can and cannot do for you. The entanglement of meaning and purpose with success restricts the natural expansion of your life. It is akin to a race dog pursuing the mechanical rabbit around a track. The dog falsely believes in its ability to catch the "prize," but it is not possible because it is not real—and they end up going nowhere.

Money is just a tool. You can make a conscious choice to give it less emotional power in your life. The following list helps you do this, by reinforcing the fact that money cannot buy the most meaningful things life has to offer.

What Money Can Buy	What Money Can't Buy
A house	A home
A bed	Sleep
Books	Intelligence
Food	An appetite
Luxury	Culture
Finery	Beauty
Medicine	Health
Flattery	Respect
Companions	Friends
Amusements	Happiness

Make Financial Decisions Jointly

Although it is true that the best things in life are not things, financial problems and problems within families are often related. After all, it is hard to enjoy life when you are worried about paying the bills.

Often it is an issue of not how much money a couple has but how they manage their money. In looking at Figure 5.3, notice that happy couples have significantly less financial issues than do unhappy couples, and most of the issues have to do with how financial decisions are made.

Research shows that marriages in which partners feel they have equal control over how money is spent are more satisfied with their relationship than marriages in which one partner tends to control money matters. Why is this? Money and capital represent how you define worth and how you manage the flow of energy into your daily lives. When you make money decisions together, you express equality in your partnership. Happily married couples also report a greater influence by the wife and less dominance by the husband in the handling of family finances.

Adherence to a Budget

How does a couple mutually control their money, rather than letting bills and spending control their lives? The answer is in budgeting. Budgeting does not mean cutting back on the things you really want; rather, it is a way to actively decide what you want to do with your money. It is a conscious, systematic balancing of income and expenses. Or, as one sage put it, it is a way of telling money where you want it to go instead of wondering where it went. Initially, setting a budget takes some time, but you will find it is time well spent. Developing and living within a budget can keep you out of financial trouble, as well as decrease stress in your couple relationship.

One good way to create a budget is to keep track of everything you spend money on in a given month. You may be surprised where your money goes when you put it down on paper. (At the end of this chapter a budget worksheet is provided to help you develop a working budget.)

Sticking to a budget can be difficult at first. You may need to eliminate impulse buying and really practice being disciplined with your money. Allowing a fixed amount each month for items such as gifts and entertainment makes the experience more pleasurable. Having a definite figure in mind helps you avoid spending more than you can afford. And it is a great feeling to know that you are in control of your money.

Having a budget can also help reduce conflict. As mentioned earlier in this chapter, I (Peter) am more of a saver than my wife is. Early in our marriage finances were becoming a major point of conflict. I was the one managing our money and checkbook, so at any given time, I knew more about what our financial picture looked like than Heather did. Whenever Heather wanted to purchase something, she felt as though she had to come and ask permission.

With no set budget, I had become the financial gatekeeper and was always saying no to her ideas on purchasing a gift for a friend or something nice for our home. Neither of us liked the roles into which we had slipped.

It was not until we met with an older, wiser friend for some help that we realized how helpful a clear budget could be. First, our friend had us figure out exactly what our monthly earnings and expenses were. Next, he challenged Heather to do the preliminary calculations on how much we should be saving and spending in each area per month. This brought her up to speed on our financial picture and forced me to give up some control. Finally, he had us stop using our credit cards and go to a cash-only approach. Seeing that we could pay our bills and save a little money each month met my need to feel that we were living within our means. Budgeting some spending cash for Heather allowed her to make certain purchases without feeling as if she had to ask for permission. The fact that we were only using cash gave me the confidence that we wouldn't overspend, because when the money was gone, we had to wait until the next month to replenish our spending accounts.

This system worked so well for us that we still use it twelve years later. We found that a budget could not only help us balance our spending and savings but totally reduce the conflict in this challenging area of marriage.

Plan for Savings

> "Thrift used to be a basic American virtue. Now the American virtue is to spend money."
>
> DAVID BRINKLEY

In creating a budget, you and your partner will have an opportunity to decide how much of your income to save. If you find it difficult to save money, you may want to consider having a portion taken out of your paycheck as an automatic payroll deduction. Think of this as paying yourselves first.

General wisdom says that savings should account for 10 to 25 percent of your gross income. Remember, it is never too late or too early to start saving. And money invested in a safe place at a good interest rate continues to grow steadily. Refer to Figure 5.3 again to see the results of saving just thirty dollars per month at 5 percent and 10 percent interest over time.

Reuse

Reusing products can be a money-saving strategy, with the added bonus of being environmentally friendly. Reusing is all about minimizing waste without compromising the quality of life to which we have become accustomed. Some of the strategies are: buying durable, well-constructed items that last longer, repairing items that break, buying and selling in the used marketplace, donating things that are no longer wanted or needed, refilling, refurbishing, recharging, borrowing and lending, and exchanging.

Many people currently apply the principles of reusing already: visiting libraries, reusing bags from the grocery store, renting DVDs instead of buying them. In our (Amy's) home, books and DVDs were a big expense. We became accustomed to the convenience of ordering any book we wanted and having it arrive within a few days at our doorstep. We have many bookshelves, but ultimately they have all become full. It is certainly nice to own favorite books or reference works, but the quantity of books we were accumulating began to feel overwhelming. We started visiting the library and would have long ago had we known what fun it would be. Local libraries are a fantastic resource; a fun outing, especially for children; and a great way to cut back on excess books, tapes, DVDs, CDs, and so on. Borrowing books and DVDs from the library saves our family at least fifty dollars per month, prevents unnecessary waste, and conserves the natural resources required to ship ordered books from stores.

Other reusing strategies are not as common but are excellent ways to save money and prevent the culture of excessive waste. Sharing things or resources also builds relationships within your community. Toys, books, video games, and power tools are very easy to lend. Neighborhoods can choose to co-own products such as snow blowers or lawn mowers. Sharing resources is also a great way to save money and build community relationships. Start a baby-sitting co-op in your neighborhood, if it doesn't already have one. Another idea is to trade services for like-valued ones. For example, a hair stylist I know cuts the hair for several families in exchange for piano lessons for one of her children and lawn care and snow shoveling from another family.

VOLUNTARY SIMPLICITY

The increasing number of people choosing to live simply has grown out of the recognition that we have become imprisoned by our lifestyles, material goods, and endless wants. This is sometimes referred to as the "simplicity movement" or "downshifting." Followers actively and consciously choose to reduce their consumption of products, thereby enjoying what they have more, raising its intrinsic value. They spend less time acquiring things and more time acquiring experiences, insight, and relationships. Less clutter in our surroundings frees time and energy away from maintaining those things to spending more time with family, friends, nature, or study.

While the simplicity movement is philosophical and is not principally derived from financial *need* to spend less, saving money is a positive by-product of such a lifestyle. Couples, individuals, and families can find real satisfaction in using less not only as a way to contribute less to the amount of solid waste produced but also as a way to be in control of spending. It also offers an approach to be more mindful of your consumer habits, thwarting the negative effects of materialism.

To begin with, be cognizant of your purchases. Ask yourself, "Why do I want this and what will it do? Is it a real need?" If you determine the purchase is not necessary, take some time before actually purchasing it. Sometimes this will be a few minutes; other times it may be a few days. Either way, this will prevent impulsive purchasing. You can always buy it at a later time, but often you will decide you no longer want or need the item. This is an opportunity with many rewards and few, if any, consequences, other than being less expensive and freeing time to concentrate more on special people in your life. If you don't find freedom in having less, you can always go back to purchasing products. Think of it as an experiment with nothing to lose and a lot to gain.

WHAT DO YOU *REALLY* WANT?

While budgeting, saving, paying off debt, and managing money are practical things to do, the following story beautifully illustrates the futility in our overemphasis on money. After reading this story, think about what really matters to you and then share with your partner how you would spend your days if the need to generate an income were magically removed from your life. You may find your idea of a good life is a lot simpler than you let yourself acknowledge.

A vacationing American businessman was standing on a pier in a quaint coastal fishing village in southern Mexico when a small boat with just one young fisherman pulled into the dock. Inside the small boat were several large yellowfin tuna. The American complimented the Mexican on the quality of his fish.

"How long did it take you to catch them?" the American casually asked.

"Oh, a couple hours," the Mexican replied.

"Why don't you stay out longer and catch more fish?" the American businessman then asked.

The Mexican warmly replied, "With this I have more than enough to support my family's needs."

The businessman then became serious. "But what do you do with the rest of your time?"

Responding with a smile, the Mexican fisherman answered, "I sleep late, play with my children, watch ball games, take siesta with my wife. Sometimes in the evenings I take a stroll into the village to see my friends, play the guitar, sing a few songs—"

The American businessman impatiently interrupted. "Look, I have an MBA from Harvard, and I can help you to be more profitable. You can start by fishing several hours longer every day. You can then sell the extra fish you catch. With the extra money, you can buy a bigger boat. With the additional income that larger boat will bring, you can then buy a second boat, a third one, and so on, until you have an entire fleet of fishing boats.

"Then, instead of selling your catch to a middleman you'll be able to sell your fish directly to the processor or even open your own cannery. Eventually, you could control the product, processing, and distribution. You could leave this tiny coastal village and move to Mexico City, or possibly even L.A. or New York City, where you could even further expand your enterprise."

Having never thought of such things, the Mexican fisherman asked, "But how long will all of this take?"

After a rapid mental calculation, the businessman pronounced, "Probably about fifteen to twenty years, maybe less if you work really hard."

"And then what, señor?" asked the fisherman.

"Why, that's the best part!" answered the businessman with a laugh. "When the time is right, you would sell your company stock to the public and become very rich. You would make millions."

"Millions? Really? What could I do with it all?" asked the young fisherman in disbelief.

The businessman boasted, "Then you could happily retire with all the money you've made. You could move to a quaint coastal village where you could sleep late, play with your grandchildren, watch ballgames, take siesta with your wife, and stroll to the village in the evenings where you could play the guitar and sing with your friends all you want."

CHECK-IN PROCESS

Where are you *now*? (Identify and discuss your results.)

    1. Review the Couple Checkup *individual* results. How satisfied were each of you in this area?

_____

_____

    2. Review the Couple Checkup *couple* results. Were finances a strength or growth area?

_____

_____

    3. Discuss your agreement items (your strengths).

_____

_____

Where would you like to be? (Discuss issues.)

    1. Review the discussion items in your Couple Checkup report.

    2. Choose one issue you both want to resolve.

    3. Share how you each feel about the issue.

How do you get there? (Develop your action plan.)

    1. Brainstorm a list of ways to handle your financial problems.

    2. Agree on one solution you will try.

    3. Decide what you will each do to make the plan work.

    4. Review the progress in one week.

COUPLE EXERCISE 5.1
Money: What Does It Mean to You?

1	2	3	4	5
Strongly Disagree	Disagree	Undecided	Agree	Strongly Agree

_____ 1. I look up to those people who have been very financially successful.

_____ 2. In making a major purchase, an important consideration is what others will think of my choice.

_____ 3. Having high-quality things reflects well on me.

_____ 4. It is important for me to maintain a lifestyle similar to or better than that of my peers.

_____ 5. Having some money in savings is very important to me.

_____ 6. I would rather have extra money in the bank than some new purchase.

_____ 7. I prefer safe investing with a moderate return versus high-risk investing with potentially high returns.

_____ 8. I feel more content when I know we have enough money for our bills.

_____ 9. I really enjoy shopping and buying new things.

_____ 10. People who have more money have more fun.

_____ 11. I really enjoy spending money on myself and on others.

_____ 12. Money can't buy happiness, but it sure helps.

_____ 13. He or she who controls the purse strings calls the shots.

_____ 14. It would be difficult for me to put all my money into a joint account.

_____ 15. One of the important benefits of money to me is the ability to influence others.

_____ 16. I think we each should control the money we earn.

Scoring and interpretation: After taking the quiz, add up your answers to the four questions for each category and record your scores below. Scores for each category can range from 4 to 20, with a high score indicating more agreement with that approach. It is possible to have high or low scores in more than one category.

General guidelines for scoring and interpreting your scores appear in the two boxes below. Record the interpretation for your score in each category on the scoring chart.

SCORING

Category	Add Items	Your Score
Money as status	1–4	
Money as security	5–8	
Money as enjoyment	9–12	
Money as control	13–16	

INTERPRETATION

Total Score	Score Interpretation
17–20	Very high
13–16	High
9–12	Moderate
4–8	Low

COUPLE EXERCISE 5.2
Creating a Budget

INCOME: (Take-Home Pay)		
Male:		
Female:		
Other income:		
TOTAL INCOME:		

EXPENSES: (Monthly)		Current spending	Future Budget plan
GIVING:			
HOUSING:	Rent or mortgage		
	Utilities:		
	Phone:		
LOANS/DEBT:	Car		
	Personal		
	Credit Cards		
TRANSPORTATION:	Gasoline		
	Repairs/ Maintenance		
FOOD:	Food at home		
	Food away from home		
HEALTH CARE:			
INSURANCE:	Medical		
	Car		
	Home/Life/ Health		
CLOTHING:			
PERSONAL GOODS:			
HOUSEHOLD SUPPLIES			

SERVICES:	Cell phone		
	Cable/Dish		
	Internet		
	Dry cleaning/ Laundry		
	Other		
OTHER EXPENDITURES:	Savings		
	Gifts		
	Entertainment		
	Daycare		
	Child support		
	Other		
TOTAL EXPENSES			
Surplus or deficit			

COUPLE EXERCISE 5.3
Setting Short-Term and Long-Term Goals

Individually identify your short- and long-term financial goals. Goals should be realistic and attainable. Once you and your partner have each determined three short-term and three long-term financial goals, share your goals with one another. Decide together how you can reach these goals.

For example, one goal might be to open a savings account to help with your child's (or grandchild's) college tuition. Another goal might be to buy a new home. You can then decide exactly how much money you are willing to contribute to this fund every month.

Short-Term Financial Goals

Partner 1   Partner 2

1. _____   1. _____

2. _____   2. _____

3. _____   3. _____

Long-Term Financial Goals

Partner 1	Partner 2
1. _____	1. _____
2. _____	2. _____
3. _____	3. _____

REMINDERS FOR IMPROVING YOUR FINANCES

1. Review and update your financial goals monthly.

2. Talk about what each of you value most in life and whether money relates to those values.

3. Be aware of the "hidden costs" of the goods or services you purchase (i.e., loss of or interference with couple or family time, the unavailability of those funds for something else, the extra work hours needed to pay for purchases, and so on).

4. Challenge yourselves to "no money needed" date nights. Scour the Internet for ideas if you need. These dates are often more fun and more memorable than dates that require money. Whether you decide to visit local buildings and landmarks or explore a local forest or cave, these dates are also great ways to get to know your community better.

5. Review any major debt you may have and plan how you will pay it off.

6. Talk about the spender-saver patterns in your relationship.

7. Join or form an investment club. Investment clubs are social gatherings where people share and learn about finances and investments.

8. Seek the help of a financial advisor, particularly if you have ongoing financial problems.

SIX

SEX—
BEYOND THE BIRDS
AND BEES

*Sex is a conversation carried out by other means.
If you get on well out of bed, half the problems in bed are solved.*

—PETER USTINOV

SEXUAL STRENGTHS OF HAPPY COUPLES

A major strength for happily married couples is the quality of their sexual relationship. The distinct differences found between happy and unhappy couples in terms of their sexual relationship are summarized in Figure 6.1. Individuals in happy marriages are much more satisfied with the amount of affection they receive from their partner than unhappily married couples. They also agree that their sexual relationship is satisfying and fulfilling, and they are much more likely to agree that their partner does not use or refuse sex in an unfair way. Further, they are far less likely to feel concerned that their partner is not interested in them sexually. Finally, they have few if any concerns that their partner may have thought about having a sexual relationship outside of their marriage.

FIGURE 6.1
Strengths of Happy Couples Versus Unhappy Couples
Regarding Sexuality

Sexuality Issue	Percentage in Agreement	
	Happy Couples	Unhappy Couples
1. I am completely satisfied with the affection I receive from my partner.	68%	17%
2. Our sexual relationship is satisfying and fulfilling.	76%	28%
3. My partner does not use or refuse sex in an unfair way.	82%	36%
4. I have no concerns that my partner may not be interested in me sexually.	84%	40%
5. I do not worry that my partner may consider an affair.	86%	45%

WHAT SEX REVEALS AND CONCEALS

The sexual relationship acts as an emotional barometer in that it reflects a couple's satisfaction with other aspects of their relationship. In other words, a good sexual relationship is often the outcome of a good emotional relationship between partners. While there are instances when a couple's sexual relationship suffers due to physiological or "functionality" impediments, most obstacles stem from the quality of the relationship itself. In this way, a couple's sex life can reveal the heart of the relationship.

Paradoxically, sex can also suppress and conceal deeper concerns and relationship issues. Some couples try to use sex to "smooth over" disputes. This may seem to be the easier alternative to actually talking about and working through issues, but it is never more than a temporary solution to an underlying problem.

Because sexuality affects and is affected by other aspects of a relationship, the sexual relationship tends to be a good gauge of the overall health and well-being of your marriage. Couples who have a good emotional connection have the best physical relationship. For them, sexuality flows from emotional intimacy based on open and honest communication. A marriage that is characterized by a lack of trust, stressed with financial concerns, or plagued with destructive conflict is probably not sexually satisfying for either partner.

In a classic study of 5,945 couples, researchers discovered couples who fought about such things as parenting, household responsibilities, or finances tend to have less-satisfying sexual relationships.[1] An intimate, loving, respectful sexual relationship can be a physical manifestation of all that is good and right in your marriage—your deep emotional bond, your shared values, your love for the children you may be raising together. An unsatisfying sexual relationship may be an indication that something is wrong, or at least not as right as it could be, in your relationship.

COMMON SEXUAL PROBLEMS IN RELATIONSHIPS

Sexuality is an area in which the differences between a husband's and wife's preferences are more common and problematic. Our survey revealed data on sexual issues present in all couples; Figure 6.2 summarizes the findings. Many couples are not as satisfied with their sex lives. It is not as satisfying as they would like: It may be boring. Some do not talk openly about sex. Many people express a desire for their partners to be more affectionate, yet there is an unwillingness to be affectionate due to this affection being misinterpreted as a desire for sex.

FIGURE 6.2
Top Five Sexual Problems for Couples

Sexual Issue	Percentage of Couples Having Problem*
1. I am dissatisfied with the amount of affection I receive from my partner.	68%
2. Our levels of sexual interest are different.	66%
3. Our sexual relationship has become less interesting and enjoyable.	62%
4. Our sexual relationship is not satisfying or fulfilling.	58%
5. I am dissatisfied with the level of openness in discussing sexual topics.	52%

* One or both partners indicated this was an issue for them.

MIXED MESSAGES ON SEX

The irony of sex in Western culture is that it is depicted heavily in advertising, television, movies, and magazines, yet normal sexual behavior is almost a taboo topic within cultural discourse. So, while we are bombarded with images of sex to sell products, sexual normalcy is rarely discussed, even within couple relationships.

Through advertising, corporations take a complicated emotional and physical phenomenon—sexuality—and reduce it to one-dimensional images to best sell their products. This is a "dumbing down" for consumers, because in the eyes of corporations, a good consumer is not one who thinks deeply or has their needs met through relationships and community. A good consumer must be led to believe that all human needs can be met in the marketplace: we can experience acceptance, freedom, fulfillment, and sex appeal, in a car, in the right outfit, or even with the right perfume.

Jean Kilbourne has extensively researched the harmful effects of the prevalence of sex in the media. According to Kilbourne, the negative effects "have far more to do with trivializing sex than promoting it. The problem is not that it is sinful but that it is synthetic and cynical. We are offered pseudo-sexuality that makes it far more difficult to discover our unique and authentic sexuality."[2]

Sex in media has become omnipresent. One study found that prime-time network television features sexual content every four minutes.[3] Most disturbing, they report, is that this content is almost never countered with messages of responsibility, physical consequences, or any lasting emotional impact. And the majority of young people claim that media is a major medium through which they learn about sex.[4]

When we are surrounded by distorted images of sexuality that are not countered by realistic images, it begins to control the framework for how we think about and express sexuality. This understandably can lead to problems and disappointments in our own sexual relationships. Our culture has helped set up these disappointments—from our fear of showing our bodies because they do not look like the ideal we encounter in the media, to feeling unhappy when sex fails to live up to how it is depicted in movies and on television.

It helps to bring awareness to these contrived and simplified views of sex we see. When an ad uses sex or body parts to sell, we can dissect it. Ask yourself: What are they trying to sell? Who is the population they are targeting? Realize that media images cannot embody complex human sexualities; they are fake depictions, sex stripped of its humanity. What is missing from the sex we see all around us is something that can only be found in a deep and committed relationship—sexual intimacy.

Different Levels of Sexual Interest

The movie *Annie Hall* depicts two lovers with different perceptions of their sexual relationship. When a therapist asks them (separately) how often they have sex, the character played by Woody Allen answers, "Hardly ever—maybe three times a week." The character played by Diane Keaton replies, "Constantly—three times a week."

Among married couples, one of the most common sexual concerns stems from differing interests in sex and affection. Studies have shown that for a majority of men, sex can be easily separated from the relationship. For instance, if he is angry at her for spending more time at the office than she spends at home, he is likely still interested in sex. But women tend to view sex from a relational perspective. For instance, if she is angry at him for forgetting to run some errands he had promised to take care of, she may not feel affectionate toward him. Feelings of emotional intimacy in the relationship usually precede sexual expression for women, whereas males often view sex as a way to increase intimacy.

> Jon returned home from a business trip and went straight to bed, sick with the flu for two days. That left Cheryl busy with her own job, shuttling the kids around to their activities, and trying to run a household with Jon under the weather. So she was very surprised when he initiated sex with her. She said, "I can't believe you're in the mood. You've been sick for two days, and I don't even feel like we've had time to have a conversation for over a week!" For Cheryl, making love flowed from feeling connected and close to her husband. She wanted emotional intimacy to precede their sexual connection. Jon, on the other hand, felt closer to Cheryl after they'd made love. For him, it was the road to emotional connection.

Lack of Affection from Your Partner

Spouses often are not satisfied with the amount of affection they receive from their partners. We know this is a very important component to a happy marriage because it was the highest discriminator between happily and unhappily married couples. (In 68 percent of happily married couples, partners report being satisfied with the affection they get from each other, versus only 17 percent of unhappy couples.)

When newspaper columnist Ann Landers polled her readers on their thoughts and feelings about sex, 72 percent of the ninety thousand women who responded said they'd be content to be held lovingly rather than actually have sex. Although this was not a scientifically conducted study, it certainly highlights the importance of affection. Nonsexual touch is very important to most women and many men.

Difficulty Talking about Your Sexual Relationship

The process of talking about sex and your feelings about it can be very difficult, even for married couples. One reason for this is that we have rarely had models for this type of conversation. Sex is most likely something you did not frequently discuss with your parents while growing up. When sex is talked about among adolescents, it is often misinformed, unrealistic, and immature. Because of this, mature discussions of sexual issues have acquired a taboo-like quality.

> "Love is an irresistible desire to be irresistibly desired."
>
> ROBERT FROST
> (1874–1963)

In fact, half of all married couples find it difficult to discuss sexual issues. There is a significant discrepancy between happily and unhappily married couples in the ability to discuss sexuality. In only 34 percent of unhappily married couples do partners report satisfaction in talking about sexual issues, compared with 83 percent of happily married couples. Therefore, the ability to communicate about sexual expectations and preferences is important in developing and maintaining both sexual and relational satisfaction.

Male and Female Differences

We think it is important to understand that males and females are innately different, and to explain sex differences from this perspective. In the scientific community there is, of course, no question that there are clear behavioral variations between males and females. Any dispute that may exist is over how variations come to be—the classic "nature vs. nurture" debate. Nurture proponents claim that sex differences are a result of social conditioning, but more and more biological evidence emerges on the nature side of the argument to help us understand why the average male and female are so different.

Male and female brains are organically different. The pattern of cells and structure of the hypothalamus (the part of the brain controlling sexual behavior) are distinct and different in male and female brains. In addition, hormones released during brain development in the womb further push the brain into either a male or female pattern.[5]

Since the female sex hormone estrogen helps nerve cells connect, female brain hemispheres are better connected, creating the chemical reason why women more easily multitask. These differences make sense when you consider the hunting-and-gathering cultures of our past. Females managed the home, cared for children, and gathered the bulk of the family's food. They excelled verbally and in fine motor skills. Men, on the other hand, focused on hunting, which their brains were better designed to handle since the male brain excels in visual-spatial tasks such as navigating, tracking objects, and three-dimensional problem solving. In addition, different chemicals in the male brain encourage them to seek risk.

In contemporary societies where gender equality is the decree, not realizing biological influences on behavior can cause conflict and misunderstanding. For example, since emotion is contained in the right hemisphere of the brain and speech in the opposite hemisphere, the fact that a male's brain hemispheres are not as well connected as a female's means it is biologically more difficult for men to express emotion. Women often value conversation and emotional expression from their partners and become frustrated when they don't deliver. A woman may interpret a man's lack of emotional reciprocity as lack of affection, when it actually is just something that does not come naturally to him.

Testosterone is the sex-activating hormone in both men and women. Males have more access to testosterone than women do for two reasons: First, a male's brain was exposed to high concentrations of testosterone at a critical time when his brain was taking shape as an embryo. Secondly, once a male reaches puberty, he has twenty times more testosterone in his body than a female does. These large doses of testosterone, and the fact that a male brain is best able to process information visually, predisposes males to view sex differently than a female does. This is why men can more easily separate sex from the rest of the relationship and why they are more likely to be visually stimulated in regard to sex. Women are more interested in the relational side of sex because the female brain is organized to place primacy on relationships.

So what is the relevance of biological differences between males and females to relationships? First of all, remember that statistics focus on the aggregate, but individuals vary greatly. There are always people who do not fall into the "average" group in any research. Secondly, men and women are (on average) clearly different but certainly not diametrically opposed. We have the capacity to get along, love, and solve problems. Awareness of differences, especially differences of a sexual nature, can help us suspend value judgments and set us up to respect these differences instead of trying in vain to change one another.

Let's explore these differences in the case of newlyweds Sophia and Brad. Sophia assumed she knew all about Brad sexually after a year of marriage. But when she discovered he was looking at photos of nude women, she felt as though he was betraying her. In her female brain, she interpreted this to mean that Brad had an emotional connection to the image, but to Brad it was just a graphic depiction of something that physically aroused him.

> Women are not, in the main, turned on by pictures of nudes. When they are, the sex of the nude seems to be irrelevant—they are interested in the picture for its beauty, or by identification with the figure featured. Women may be aroused by pictures of couples coupling—because what they are seeing, in however sterile a sexual context, is a relationship in action. They are not excited by a picture of a penis, while close-ups of the female genitalia do arouse men.[6]

Brad and Sophia were able to sidestep bad feelings, in part because they both learned how the sexual natures of men and women are often very different. Sophia realized she didn't have to take it personally when Brad was tempted to view sexually explicit material. At the same time, Brad realized how intertwined emotional, relational, and sexual intimacy was for Sophia. He stopped looking at nude photos of women, and they began to work on ways to increase the intimacy in their own marriage.

WAYS TO CREATE MORE SEXUAL INTIMACY

The following are ways to improve your sexual relationship . . . thereby improving your overall couple relationship.

Improve Communication

Different people have different needs for sexual intimacy, and those needs affect how they perceive their sexual behavior. So couples must communicate clearly about sex if they are to maintain a satisfying relationship. Communication will facilitate an understanding of your partner's perspective and levels of sexual interest, which will strengthen your bond and increase the intimacy between you.

The quality of your communication affects the quality of your relationship, and the quality of your relationship affects the quality of the sex. You need to talk. You need to listen, early and often. If you find your lives are so scheduled with work and family commitments that you don't have time to talk and listen to your spouse, sit down and schedule time. Meaningful conversation needs to take priority over television, the newspaper, the Internet, and other distractions. It links you to your partner—it's both a cause and effect of a loving, respectful sexual relationship. If you are not communicating naturally, work on doing it unnaturally until it becomes second nature. Don't worry if it feels contrived at first. If communicating about sex feels very uncomfortable and awkward, it is a good indicator of the need for it.

For tips on how to improve communication skills, refer back to chapter 3. Active listening and "I" statements can help guide you through sensitive issues about sex. "I" statements are more effective than "You" statements, especially in matters related to sex. Additionally, self-disclosure—an intimate act in and of itself—leads to intimacy, plain and simple. Generally sharing your deepest hopes, fears, and dreams with your partner will help you learn to share your feelings and desires about sex too.

Nonverbal communication is also important, especially in regard to sex. Touch and eye contact are two ways to communicate warmth and affection. There is probably no better time to put body language to use than when the subject is sex.

Since he has started his own business, Jim has been stressed, tired, and busier than ever. Working those long hours only to come home in a bad mood has taken a toll on his and Julie's relationship. In the last six months, they have had more conflict in their marriage than the first eight years combined. They also have not been sexually intimate in over three months.

Julie tried to get Jim to talk about what was on his mind. She asked him to share what was causing him so much stress, but he ascribed to the idea that "work should stay at work." So his tough veneer, characterized by a lack of communication and grumpy mood, only pushed Julie further away, leaving them feeling distant and cold. Jim justified his position by stating he didn't want to burden the rest of the family with his problems.

One day, Jim finally opened up and told her about his fear of failing as a business owner. It had been a big risk for him to leave the security of his former job to go out on his own. And to make matters worse, he could still hear his father's words from years earlier stating that "he'd never amount to anything." As Jim opened up about his feelings, Julie was drawn in. She held him as he spoke, listened, and shed tears with him over the pain he'd been carrying. In the end, sharing his innermost thoughts and feelings was not a burden for Julie; it was a gift that drew them closer together and only increased their love and connection. There were still days that Jim was stressed, but their conflict decreased and their sexual activity increased to normal levels again.

For Jim and Julie, self-disclosure increased their levels of emotional and physical intimacy.

Give Tokens of Affection

If you think back to the early stages of your relationship with your spouse, you may remember that giving and sharing seemed to be easy. You probably shared more positive feelings and experiences than negative ones, and you probably found many ways to express love and affection. These "tokens of affection" are just as important now as they were then. This can be as simple as calling in the middle of the day to let your partner know you are thinking of him or her.

After all, the people in your life you enjoy being around most likely make you feel valued and accepted. The following example illustrates how we tend to like people who make us feel special:

> A young woman was explaining to a friend why she had decided to marry one man rather than another. "When I was with John," she said, "I felt he was the cleverest person in the world."
>
> "Then why didn't you choose him?" the puzzled friend asked.
>
> "Because when I'm with Bill I feel I'm the cleverest person in the world."[7]

You may have to consciously remind yourself to give these tokens of affection—compliments, little gifts, cards, and so on. These things make a difference precisely because they are little things, and little things count big in taking the emotional temperature of your relationship. Giving and receiving unexpected favors, compliments, and help are the things that warm you toward your spouse. They keep you in an open, loving frame of mind. Added up together, they demonstrate constancy and affection. They show you care.

Feeling cared for and loved are essential emotions for a meaningful sexual relationship. When you make a focused effort to do small daily things for your partner, you make him or her feel special and valued. Many of us forget this after years in a relationship. To get back in the habit, you may have to make a deliberate effort to give these tokens of affection. But by doing so, you will soon discover the reciprocal nature of giving: your relationship will deepen far beyond the value of the tokens you offer. You never lose by giving. And soon it will be natural and easy again. You and your partner can only gain greater love and intimacy when you give to each other.

In his book *The Five Love Languages*, Dr. Gary Chapman talks about the different ways each person prefers to give and receive love. These include: acts of service, quality time, touch, words of affection, and gifts. His approach suggests that we often make the mistake of speaking our own "love language" to our partner, when he or she really prefers to receive love in another way.[8] A quick conversation can usually help couples determine their primary love language and begin to be more deliberate about expressing love and affection in a way that will be most meaningful to their partner. To determine your partner's primary love language, take note of how she/he expresses love toward others.

Also, pay attention to what they typically ask for. These are clues to what their love language is and what they may like to receive from you.

Understand Differences in Desire

Judge James Sheridan, in his book *A Blessing for the Heart*, advises married couples to not let different levels of desire stop them from experiencing romance and sex. He says God intended for man and woman to be different, and therefore acts of love will always call for elements of sacrifice. He explains, "There would be no real sacrifice if both you and your spouse always wanted the identical thing at the identical time. It is the sacrifice of giving that gives love meaning."[9]

Men and women will always be different—it is these differences that attract us in the first place, and ironi-

> "My wife is a sex object. Every time I ask for sex, she objects."
>
> LES DAWSON

cally, these differences often drive couples apart later. There may be times when you will have sex just to please your partner, but begrudgingly surrendering to sex as an obligation will not build intimacy. Demanding sex or pouting when it doesn't happen does not build intimacy either. If saying yes to sex is putting your partner's needs above your own, it must be done to affirm your love and accept your partner's love; otherwise, the only thing you will build is resentment.

About 80 percent of married couples report that the husbands want sex more than the wives do, but some researchers believe this may have more to do with the fact that our culture tends to define desire by the initiation of sex.[10] Debra Taylor and Michael Sytsma found that women experience a receptive type of sexual desire that is triggered once sexual activity begins. They claim that most women will respond positively to sexual advances; they are just biologically less likely to think about it in the first place. Understanding these differences makes it easier for men to accept the fact that they may be the ones to initiate sex most often. Viewed through this framework of biological differences, the failure to initiate sex does not reflect poorly on a relationship; it is just a difference in the way men and women are designed.

WHEN THE RELATIONSHIP ISN'T THE PROBLEM

Sexual problems do not always stem from interpersonal or relational issues. Sometimes sexual problems are caused by physical conditions, reactions to medication, or intrapsychic problems. Pioneer sex researchers William Masters and Virginia Johnson found that physiological sex-based problems account for 10 to 20 percent of all sexual problems. For example, according to research, up to 80 percent of erectile dysfunction has an organic cause, such as cardiovascular disease or diabetes.[11]

Side effects of certain medications, such as antidepressants or blood pressure medications, can affect sexual desire and function. Hormone imbalances are also responsible for physical aspects of dysfunction as well as low libido. And deeper psychological issues, such as depression, guilt, and effects of past sexual trauma, are examples of intrapsychic problems that can affect sexuality. Physical and lifestyle factors that can cause physical sexual problems are smoking, obesity, and alcoholism.

These are only some possible physical causes of sexual problems. While we have primarily discussed relationship issues as they relate to sexual intimacy, it is important to be aware of the possibility of a physical cause—either primary or secondary—of sexual problems. If you suspect a physical origin to your sexual problems, seek the advice of a physician or trained sex-therapy professional. A determination can be made as to whether or not there is an organic source, such as a deficiency of sex hormone levels. An accurate diagnosis is necessary for developing an appropriate treatment plan. Treatment can include medication, hormones, anxiety reduction techniques, and sex therapy and general relationship enhancement.

INTIMACY AND DIFFERENTIATION

Many of the apparent physiological impediments to sex actually have a deeper origin. If you watch television, you will have noticed drug company advertisements for medications that supposedly aid couples in the sex act. These advertisements often make psychologists and therapists cringe, because they realize physiological adequacy rarely translates into satisfying sex. These advertisements insinuate that all you need for a great sex life is the physical ability to perform intercourse. They do nothing to address the issues of desire, passion, intimacy, and attraction.

According to Psychologist David Schnarch, "Modern sexology has confused sexual performance with the inner experience of sexuality, overlooking considerations of eroticism, desire, and personal meaning."[12] Schnarch asserts standard sex therapy practices are ineffective because they fail to address the underlying cause of sexual problems: a person's lack of differentiation. *Differentiation* refers to the ability to remain oneself in the face of group influences. A highly differentiated person is able to stay connected with others while making independent decisions. They can support and accept another's viewpoint while making independent decisions, or they can reject another's viewpoint without polarizing their differences.

By contrast, an undifferentiated person has no internal stable "self" and relies so heavily on the approval of others, they will adjust what they say, do, or even think in order to agree with another. Disagreement is threatening to their fragile sense of self. Other ways undifferentiated people define themselves or gain approval are by pressuring others to agree with them (bullying) or by routinely opposing the positions of others (rebelling).

Schnarch's therapeutic approach to sexual intimacy is for each individual to engage in this process of becoming differentiated. The centerpiece of this task is to tolerate and manage the unavoidable anxiety one experiences when revealing his true self. He contends that avoiding anxiety is what prevents genuine intimacy and gratifying sex. Selectively sharing pieces of yourself based on what you perceive your partner will respond to favorably is easy. But to be deeply known by your partner "requires the courage, integrity, and maturity to face oneself and, even more frightening, convey that self—all that one is capable of feeling and experiencing—to the partner."[13]

POSITIVE ACTION

If you find that your relationship has lost the spark it once had, you will need to make a conscious, focused effort to increase its emotional and physical temperature. When it comes to taking action in terms of implementing these ideas into your lives, just do it! Give your spouse a genuine compliment, hold his hand, leave a no-occasion note. Every day, go out of your way to do something kind and affectionate.

> "More people behave themselves into new ways of thinking than think themselves into new ways of behaving."
>
> UNKNOWN

You may be surprised to find that, by changing your actions or your motions, your emotions will change as well. We often make the mistake of believing that we have to have the feeling before we can take the action. This is not necessary.

In fact, by changing your actions, you will also change your emotions. Sexual intimacy is not something that is achieved once, remaining constant throughout the life of a relationship. It can be acquired, lost, and regained again. But just as most things in life start with *doing*, sexual intimacy begins by spending time together, as well as making efforts during times apart to let your partner know he or she is held warmly in your thoughts. Once you get back into the habit of making your spouse feel valued and special, it will feel natural. Like anything of importance, this takes some conscious effort, but the results are worthwhile.

SUGGESTIONS FOR IMPROVING YOUR SEXUAL HEALTH

1. Always remember that good sex begins while your clothes are still on.
2. Take time to think about yourself as a sexual being.
3. Take responsibility for your own sexual pleasure.
4. Talk with your partner about sex.
5. Make time to be together regularly.
6. Don't let sex become routine in your marriage.
7. Be creative—you'll find it's one of the best aphrodisiacs.

8. Understand that working at sex doesn't work.

9. Don't carry anger into your bedroom.

10. Realize that good sex isn't just a matter of pushing the right buttons.

11. Nurture the romance in your life.

12. Don't make sex too serious.

13. Don't always wait to be "in the mood" before agreeing to have sex.

14. Realize that you and your partner don't have to see eye to eye sexually.

15. Don't be afraid to ask for help.

16. Try to keep your sexual expectations realistic.[14]

CHECK-IN PROCESS

Where are you *now*? (Identify and discuss your results.)

1. Review the Couple Checkup *individual* results. How satisfied were each of you in this area?

_____

_____

2. Review the Couple Checkup *couple* results. Was communication a strength or growth area?

_____

_____

3. Discuss your agreement items (your strengths).

_____

_____

Where would you like to be? (Discuss issues.)

1. Review the discussion items in your Couple Checkup report.

2. Choose one issue you both want to resolve.

3. Share how you each feel about the issue.

How do you get there? (Develop your action plan.)

1. Brainstorm a list of ways to handle your communication problems.

2. Agree on one solution you will try.

3. Decide what you will each do to make the plan work.

4. Review the progress in one week.

COUPLE EXERCISE 6.1
What Makes You Feel Loved?

For this exercise, take turns completing this sentence: "I feel loved when . . ."

Go back and forth, thinking and talking about those things you really appreciate and that help you experience love from your partner. Your list might include extravagant romantic items ("I feel loved when you surprise me with an anniversary trip for two"), as well as everyday gestures ("I feel loved when you wash the dishes"). Try to come up with at least ten things each. This will give both of you several options for ways to communicate love to your partner.

Remember, you're not making a "to-do list." This is a list of opportunities for you to better understand and meet one another's needs and desires.

I feel loved when . . .

_____   _____

_____   _____

_____   _____

_____   _____

_____   _____

_____   _____

_____   _____

_____   _____

_____   _____

COUPLE EXERCISE 6.2
Plan a Romantic Adventure

Make a plan to spend some quality time together. This "adventure" can be whatever pleases both of you and fits into your lives and interests. Schedule and organize this in advance, following these guidelines:

1. Be realistic.
2. Plan something you will be able to do in the next few months.
3. Plan something that is not too expensive.
4. Answer these questions:
   - When?

   _____

   _____

   - Where?

   _____

   _____

   - What can you each contribute to make it happen?

   _____

   _____

REMINDERS FOR IMPROVING
YOUR SEXUAL RELATIONSHIP

1. Remember the importance of being affectionate aside from being sexual (especially if you are a man wanting to please a woman).

2. Remember that it is OK to have sex just for the sake of sex (especially if you are a woman wanting to please a man).

3. Resolve underlying conflicts that will spill over into your sexual relationship.

4. Discuss your different levels of sexual interest.

5. Let your partner know he or she is valued and appreciated.

6. Learn to critically decipher sexualized advertising. What is being sold? What is the message? Who is the ad targeting? Do the models look like real people?

7. Keep physically fit—exercise, stop smoking, maintain healthy weight and cholesterol levels.

8. Remember that improving your emotional connection with your partner will consequently improve your physical connection.

SEVEN

ROLES— TRADITIONS, TRENDS, AND TEAMWORK

Throughout history the more complex activities have been defined and redefined, now as male, now as female, sometimes as drawing equally on the gifts of both sexes. When an activity to which each sex could have contributed is limited to one sex, a rich, differentiated quality is lost from the activity itself.

—MARGARET MEAD (1901–1978)

STRENGTHS OF HAPPY COUPLES REGARDING ROLES

Happy couples have a more balanced relationship in terms of *roles* than do unhappy couples. This claim is clearly supported data based on fifty thousand married couples whose ENRICH marriage satisfaction scale was analyzed in relation to their individual scores on roles within a marriage (Figure 7.1 summarizes the results). Two characteristics of happy couples are that the husband is as willing as the wife to adjust and that both husband and wife work toward having an equal relationship. In egalitarian relationships, both the husband and wife make adjustments to handle an issue, such as who will pick up a child who became sick at school.

FIGURE 7.1

How Happy Couples Versus Unhappy Couples View Their Roles

Role Issue	Percentage in Agreement	
	Happy Couples	Unhappy Couples
1. Both are equally willing to make adjustments in their marriage.	82%	46%
2. Both work hard to have an equal relationship.	87%	54%
3. Both are satisfied with division of housework.	76%	42%
4. The couple makes most decisions jointly.	87%	59%
5. Household tasks are divided based on preferences, not tradition.	67%	55%

A LOADED TOPIC

Roles relate to how couples allocate leadership responsibilities and household tasks. One may think that assigning roles within a marriage may be clear-cut, but in reality it is laden with expectations from numerous sources, making it an extremely complex subject. First of all, marital roles are affected by religious and cultural trends, so roles must be analyzed in specific sociocultural and historical contexts. To complicate matters, we have our own ideas of what different roles signify, collectively and as individual men and women. These ideas exist on three different levels: macro, meso, and micro. On the macro level, roles are defined through the dominant social and cultural context in which we live. The meso level is where the question of roles is resolved in our relationship. On the micro level are the feelings and opinions individual men and women have about their roles.

The scope of this book is not to recapitulate the history of marital roles and gender ideology. Its purpose is to use present-day research among present-day couples to investigate how their views and management of roles affect the quality of their relationships. This will certainly be a fallible attempt, and will likely be only relevant at this time in history. We will, however, consider the present socio-cultural and historical context, because a family exists within this context. In many ways, a family or a marriage is like a little microcosm of the larger world.

We live in a unique, historic time when it comes to gender ideology and roles within marriage. There is a diverse set of beliefs and expectations, originating from families that represent (or at one time represented) these diversities. An individual born in the 1940s or '50s, for example, will be statistically more likely to have been parented in what we term "traditional" family role relationships. In a traditional marriage, the woman is primarily responsible for taking care of the household and the children. The wife may not have worked outside the home; if she did, the man's career likely took precedence over hers. And while she may have been responsible for the household, major decision making would have been more of the husband and father's responsibility.

In recent times, people have been raised in families where both parents had careers, single-parent families, or a combination of several different family constitutions. The roles that an individual's parents played could have been determined by their biology or by their ability and willingness to perform these roles.

How roles were modeled for you as you were growing up may be arbitrary, or it may be a sign of the times in which you were born. While that model may inhabit a space in your expectations and desires, the most important factor for your personal and couple happiness is what you consider to be equitable and fair. We are going to assume a humanistic stance of equality of conditions, opportunity, and treatment. In fact, this principle exists in most all religious groups, as well as in nontheistic ethical systems: the ethic of reciprocity. This is simply the concept that we should treat others as we would want them to treat us. Christianity expresses this as the Golden Rule. It is a basic moral principle. We recognize that in a given society at a certain time, all human beings are not politically or economically equal. But by nature all human beings are of equal worth simply because they are human. This is the stance that needs to be upheld in a marriage if it is to serve both individuals.

IT'S ABOUT POWER

> "All animals are equal, but some animals are more equal than others."
>
> GEORGE ORWELL

One issue closely related to role allocation is power. Power can be a major impediment to the achievement of marital equality. According to one classic model, power in a relationship can be divided in four basic ways: (1) a husband-dominated power pattern, in which the man is basically the boss; (2) a wife-dominated power pattern, in which the woman is basically the boss; (3) an egalitarian power pattern, in which authority is shared and decisions are made on a joint basis in most areas; and (4) an autonomic power pattern, in which each spouse has essentially equal authority but in different areas of life, so they make decisions in their particular domains independent of each other. These patterns are illustrated in Figure 7.2.

Janice Steil and Beth Turetsky studied 815 dual-career couples to investigate the relationship between marital power and psychological well-being. They found that patterns of power in marriage are closely related to individual and couple well-being. For example, marriages based on equality are correlated with greater relationship satisfaction, more sincere and shared types of influence, less depression (particularly for women), and increased intimacy for both partners.[1]

In contrast, inequality affects both partners negatively. Inequality for the more powerful partner results in less relationship satisfaction, sincerity, and intimacy. For the partner with less power, consequences include low self-esteem, depression, dependency, and hostility toward the other partner.

Marital satisfaction and intimacy are much more likely when partners share responsibilities and decision making. Having a choice about who performs what

FIGURE 7.2

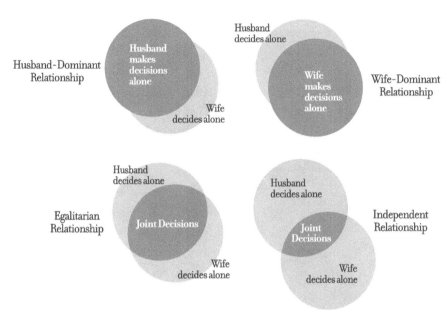

task is also an important aspect of marital satisfaction. Partners who have an egalitarian power pattern tend to be more involved and happier with each other. They are less likely to assign blame because they accept more responsibility for each other's happiness. They also tend to make better decisions because their decisions are based on the wisdom and perspective of two people.

A marriage often reproduces the power patterns that its partners witnessed as children; so individuals whose families modeled inequality in power and role relations may find it initially more difficult to relate equally to one another. In this case, both partners need to work hard on communicating positively and achieving a fair and equal partnership. In the past, most marriages were traditional, and it was hard to conceptualize an equal marriage because it was not modeled in life.

COMMON ROLE PROBLEMS

Let's take a brief look at the role issues that cause problems for a majority of couples.

UNFAIR DIVISION OF HOUSEWORK

The 1960s feminist movement catapulted women into the workforce. Women were told they could "have it all"—a fulfilling career and a family. While the feminist movement changed the workplace to accept women, the patriarchal family structure remained largely untouched, leaving women to bear the majority of housework and childcare duties. Sociologist Arlie Hochschild's 1989 research and book *The Second Shift* coined a phrase that described, and still describes, many working women's lives. They return home from their jobs within the general economy, only to be faced with their second job of maintaining a household and raising children.[2]

> "Every man is dishonest who lives upon the labor of others, no matter if he occupies a throne."
>
> ROBERT GREEN INGERSOLL

While many husbands recognize the hectic demands placed on working wives and assist with the household chores, others are oblivious or simply resist helping. Women clearly have been the recipients of an unfair division of labor in the home. In fact, in only 20 percent of dual-career marriages in Hochschild's study did the husbands share housework equally with their wives. This adds up to a lot of extra work for the average woman. Over the course of one year, an average woman will work an extra month of twenty-four-hour days just on household tasks.[3]

One study found that single mothers spend an average of sixteen hours per week on chores, while married mothers spend an average of twenty hours per week.[4] This has caused some researchers to conclude that, for many husbands, their major contribution toward the household is to create more mess. This dual labor by women in both the general economy and within the household is not good for them or their marriages. Women who try to "do it all" tend to suffer from chronic exhaustion, have a low sex drive, and get sick more frequently. These problems impact the dynamics and vitality of a marriage.

Falling into Tradition

Victoria and John were married two years before the birth of their daughter, Carolyn. Prior to Carolyn's birth, Victoria worked as a professor at a small university and John worked as a scientist for a large pharmaceutical company. The university provided Victoria with six weeks of paid maternity leave, with an additional option of six weeks' unpaid leave. Victoria took advantage of the full twelve weeks with Carolyn before hiring part-time care for her. Since her professorship allows more flexibility than John's job, she taught one of her courses two evenings a week and rearranged her office hours to be home with Carolyn more.

Quietly, Victoria began to resent how John was able to become a parent and have his professional life remain untouched. She, on the other hand, was the one arranging care, communicating with the nanny, and shuffling her work schedule to accommodate doctor appointments and days when Carolyn was sick. Additionally, her being the one at home more often shifted their relatively equally shared home responsibilities to more "traditional" roles. In the past, if John needed to work late he would let Victoria know, and she might also choose to stay and get some work done at the university, go to a yoga class, or meet with a colleague or friend. Now John's working late meant that Victoria still needed to get home to relieve the nanny; then she felt the added responsibility to prepare a meal. In addition, her social and recreational life is restricted by the need to be at home. Instead of attending her yoga class, Victoria tries to practice some yoga at home with the baby; she has less time for friends and colleagues and, ultimately, for work.

Victoria and John's situation may sound proverbial, because it is often what happens in marriages after children are born. Even marriages in which domestic tasks are split fifty-fifty, after the birth of a child, will become more traditional in terms of roles. In our study of fifty thousand couples, 44 percent reported problems stemming from the fact that housework is based on traditional roles rather than on individual interests. The risk to Victoria and to John is the following scenario: Victoria feels as though she is making all the accommodations. She is so focused on—primarily—the baby, and secondarily, her job, with her energies dissipated, that she does not have the energy to discuss with John how unfair this situation has become.

As Professor Carol Gilligan discusses in her book *In a Different Voice*, women are so focused on maintaining order and connection in relationships that they give up their voice in order to keep the peace. According to Gilligan, this self-less behavior on the part of women is maintained by our patriarchal society.[5] A monumental problem occurs when women continually act selflessly: they disconnect from the relationship. An attempt to ignore their own wishes and desires—their own voice—leads, according to Gilligan, to dissociation with their true self and a disappearance from the relationship. And a marriage cannot be satisfying or real if one member is stuffing down their feelings and needs, rendering them psychologically absent.

Even if you do not believe that giving up her needs will cause a woman to dissociate, just think about the pattern of tradition from an equality standpoint. Many couples try to dismiss roles and household responsibilities as trivial matters that do not threaten their relationship, but the truth is that role allocation profoundly influences the quality of a marriage. Although roles may seem trivial, the sheer amount of time that they demand can make them larger than life. In addition, the consequences of how roles are divided are not trivial. In researching six hundred couples filing for divorce, George Levinger found that "neglect of home and children" was second only to "mental cruelty" as the reason cited for divorce.[6] The roles taken in a marriage also tell a lot about the power dynamics in the relationship and are a symbol of relational equality.

Figure 7.3 lists the top five role issues based on our national survey.

FIGURE 7.3
Top Five Role Problems for Couples

Role Issue	Percentage of Couples Having Problem*
1. Concern about unfair division of housework.	49%
2. Housework is based on traditional roles rather than interests.	44%
3. The husband is not willing to adjust as much as the wife is.	44%

4. Disagree whether or not the wife should work outside the home when children are young.	**43%**
5. Partners disagree that both work to maintain an egalitarian relationship.	**36%**

* *One or both partners indicated this was an issue for them.*

HOW ROLES RELATE TO MARITAL SATISFACTION

When it comes to traditional roles and the happiness and vitality of a marriage, it appears that the "good old days" may not have been so good after all. As Figure 7.4 shows, an individual's perception of his relationship roles is significantly related to his partner's marital satisfaction. As in previous chapters, happy and unhappy couples were compared. This time the focus was on the type of role relationship they each had established.

A clear finding was that couples who perceive their relationship as traditional in terms of roles are much more likely to be unhappy than couples who perceive their relationship as egalitarian. If both people perceive their relationship as traditional, more than four-fifths of them are unhappy with their marriage, leaving less than one-fifth happy. Similarly, when both people perceive their relationship as egalitarian, more than four-fifths have a happy marriage, while less than one-fifth are unhappy.

For couples in which the woman perceives the relationship as traditional and the male views it as egalitarian, almost two-thirds are unhappy. If the husband perceives the relationship as traditional and the wife perceives it as egalitarian, an equal percentage of the couples are happy and unhappy.

FIGURE 7.4

Role Relationships in Happy Couples Versus Unhappy Couples

Perception of Relationship	Percentage in Agreement	
	Happy Couples	Unhappy Couples
Both perceive as egalitarian.	81%	19%
Husband perceives as traditional wife perceives as egalitarian.	50%	50%
Wife perceives as traditional, husband perceives as egalitarian.	37%	63%
Both perceive as traditional.	18%	82%

So, the more equal the woman perceives the role relationship, the happier the marriage. This analysis concurs with other research in demonstrating how the woman's perception of equality is more strongly associated to the happiness of a marriage. In addition, research has found that women may be more accurate in their reports of who does what in a household. James Thorton surveyed 555 married people and found that men tend to overestimate what they do around the household, while women underestimate all they do.[7]

LOOKS CAN BE DECEIVING

It is important to note that relationship roles can be measured not only by the external chores and duties each partner adopts but also by the internal dynamics of decision making and attitudes. From the outside, it appears that Heather and I (Peter) have very traditional relationship roles. Internally, however, we adopt very egalitarian attitudes and practices.

Heather stays at home full-time with our three young children. She does the majority of the cooking and cleaning around the house, as well as shuttling the kids from one activity to the next. I, on the other hand, would be considered the traditional breadwinner, working full-time in my career as a psychologist. By most definitions, we would be categorized as a traditional couple.

A closer look, however, paints a different picture. We make all major decisions together as a team. I place a high value on my wife's opinions and feelings, as she does mine. We have a mutual respect for one another that is supported by the belief that we have equal value and are called to love and serve one another mutually. Heather has her bachelor's degree in education, as well as a master's degree in psychology. She is at home with the kids by choice, considering it a privilege to parent them each day.

Further, we are both willing to adjust to the ever-changing demands of life. When I was in graduate school, it was my job to do the laundry each Friday because Heather was working and I had no classes that day. Later, Heather went to graduate school while I was an intern. At this point in our lives, we shared the laundry responsibilities in our home. After we had children, Heather took over the laundry because she was at home full-time and I was at work full-time. This is just one example of how our roles continue to adjust to the different stages and phases of life.

HOW TO IMPROVE YOUR ROLE RELATIONSHIP

The following are ways to improve your role relationship . . . thereby improving your overall relationship.

Men and Women Both Need to Be Part of the Solution

Wives' roles have expanded considerably in recent decades while husbands' roles have remained quite stable. The majority (56 percent) of mothers are employed, and women make up almost half of the workforce. Yet women still assume a disproportionate responsibility for the work of relationships, the home, and children.

Women typically act as facilitators of change in relationships, yet this inequality in the home has changed very little over the past thirty years. Why? In some cases, women may be sending mixed messages to men. Although they may be exhausted from and irritated by excessive responsibilities, they do not want to give up the control they have in the home. Women may have a hard time surrendering some of their responsibilities to their husbands because so much of their identities are tied to home and children, just as a man's identity is stereotypically tied to his work. Therefore, many men find that when they try to do their share of housekeeping and child care, they are critiqued and judged by their wives to the point of feeling discouraged. To develop new roles, fathers need the support of mothers.

Divide . . . and Then Stay out of It!

After roles have been divvied up equitably, do not get involved in your spouse's responsibilities unless you are asked. This requires some letting go— for perfectionist types, it may require *a lot* of letting go! But you absolutely *must* resist getting involved, or else you are not fully detaching from that role. Julie Shields, author of *How to Avoid the Mommy Trap*, wisely advises mothers as they hand over parenting tasks to fathers:

> Mom doesn't leave instructions or telephone to give guidance about junior. Dad has to deal with the situation on his own. If you do it any other way, the man becomes the helper or subcontractor, and guess who gets promoted to management, with the ultimate responsibility for seeing or doing anything that needs to get done?[8]

When you feel tempted to oversee and comment on your partner's task, *do not!* Ask yourself, "What is the worst thing that can happen if I don't interfere? As long as the health and safety of all are uncompromised, you will need to just take a deep breath and let it go. If the task has to do with childrearing, unleash the idea that it should be done as you would, and you will let go of much self-induced tension and anxiety. Of course, your spouse will parent differently—they are not you! They will have a unique parenting style and a unique relationship with the child, from which your child will benefit. If the job you have given up is taking out the garbage, and the wastebaskets have not been emptied the evening before the garbage is to be picked up, do not remind your spouse. This is patronizing and, again, puts you in the role of superior, manager, or one who is ultimately responsible. Sometimes people need to feel a consequence before a lesson is learned. Maybe the garbage sits around for an extra week. Annoying? You bet! But do not cave in and divert the responsibility back to you.

Dividing responsibilities fairly will likely mean a lowering of standards by one or both partners. For example, in Cindy and Vin's marriage, Vin does most of the cooking, because he enjoys it and is an excellent cook. Cindy and their two children have become accustomed to varied and thoughtfully planned menus most evenings—fresh and healthy meals, bordering on gourmet. And since Vin does the cooking, he also plans the meals and grocery shops, which, he admits, add up to a lot of hours of work. Cindy and Vin have decided that, while appreciated and enjoyed, Vin will cook three nights a week instead of the six nights he has been preparing meals. Cindy will be responsible for preparing meals three evenings, leaving one evening per week to dine out.

In order for this plan to be successful, Vin, the "foodie" of the family, realizes he may need to lower his expectations of his idea of a family dinner. While he would not choose boiled pasta and marinara sauce from a jar, he must not criticize if Cindy chooses such a meal for the family. Vin, in this situation, needs to realize that he has a higher standard when it comes to family dinners, and that he can exert his creativity on the evenings he cooks. On the evenings when Cindy cooks, he can enjoy a meal he did not prepare, as well as the extra time it frees for him and the family.

Forget about "Helping"

The fact that husbands often refer to doing household tasks or child care as "helping" their spouse shows how inequity is embedded in our language and thought system. Helping someone out implies the job is that person's responsibility in the first place. In his humorous and useful book *Chore Wars*, Jim Thorton addresses this point nicely:

> If there is one word that makes working women cringe, it's probably this one: Help. As in "Let me help with the chores, honey." To most of us fellows, such a comment merely epitomizes our nice-guy, decent natures. But to many women, what they really hear is this: "We both know these chores are your ultimate responsibility, dear, but if you spell out exactly what you want me to do, I will begrudgingly help you with your work. And, by the way, you better show me some appreciation for my help. And if you want me to help again,

you will have to remind me each and every single occasion this obnoxious task comes up."[9]

> "Women have convinced ourselves that we can do what men can do. But we haven't convinced ourselves, and therefore we haven't convinced our country, that men can do what women can do."
>
> GLORIA STEINEM

Remember: your marriage is a partnership. Having balance and fairness in terms of household chores and child-rearing clearly benefits your relationship. You also have a good opportunity to positively impact your relationship and your children by modeling equality.

I (Amy) have a lot of compassion for couples struggling with dividing household chores, because it has been something I struggle with personally and, at times, relationally. I was raised in an immaculately clean and organized household, so my preference and expectation is that my home should be very clean and very organized. I get a deep feeling of contentment when my home is clean. I don't even need to be home to feel this way—just knowing my home is clean conjures happiness inside me. My children have noticed after I wash and organize a cupboard or closet, I will open that cupboard for no other reason than to get the satisfaction of seeing it so clean and organized. They like to tease me by pulling up a chair, opening the cupboards, and acting as though they are as engrossed in the cupboard as they would be in a good book. This being said, you can probably understand how my love for cleanliness could slip into a pathological or, at least, an unhealthy preference!

My husband is tidy, but he does not like to clean bathrooms, floors, or windows. Because I have a lower threshold for what is considered clean, I am not only the one apt to notice a mess but also the one more bothered by it. Consequently, I have done most of the cleaning in our marriage, and through repetition and perfectionist standards, I have become very good at it. I have even been known to refold clothing on the rare occasion my husband does laundry.

Even though I realize my behavior is partially responsible for creating the imbalance, I have often resented how the cleaning chores become solely my responsibility. I initially tried some passive-aggressive tactics: not cleaning the few areas my husband and I didn't share (his sink and his shower), as well as cleaning during the times that were to be reserved as couple time. These tactics didn't work. My husband didn't seem to notice his sink and shower were dirty . . . I think it bothered me more than him. Cleaning floors instead of cuddling with my husband while watching a movie only caused me to feel irritated, and it was a loss for our relationship.

We actually used the ten-step model described in chapter 4 as a guide through this problem. The ten-step model illuminated some of the complexities of this issue for us. For example, in step 4 where we list past attempts to resolve the issue, we talked about two times in the past when we tried to hire someone to clean biweekly. According to my husband, he thought this would have been a quick fix to the problem. For me it was much more complicated. I have a difficult time hiring someone to do something I feel is our responsibility. To add to it, I expected it to be cleaned the way I would clean, and I was not happy with the results. These two attitudes together have ensured my role as housecleaning specialist!

In our brainstorming ideas, we addressed the inequity of household responsibilities as well as my perfectionist ideals. The result is that now our home is not nearly as clean and organized as I would prefer, but I recognize that my desire for *clean* is larger than the amount of time I am willing or able to devote to cleaning. Cognitively I have made *clean* less important by enjoying all the things we do at home, instead of focusing on how clean it feels.

We have also been trying a few ideas that have worked really well so far. The kids are in charge of their bedrooms and bathroom. My husband is in charge of his sink and shower. On Saturday mornings we all spend an hour cleaning and organizing. I normally assign the projects, since I "notice" more than anyone else what needs to be done. With multiple people cleaning for a full hour, a lot gets done. We turn on some good music, then often play tennis afterward and eat at a favorite Indian restaurant. If feels like a great way to start a Saturday and frees the day for anything else. I am also considering hiring outside help again, with lower expectations and the knowledge that I actually enjoy cleaning when it doesn't feel like one big overwhelming and continuous chore. Our plan is still a work in progress but feels encouraging and proactive.

Have a Plan

> "Change does not necessarily assure progress, but progress implacably requires change."
>
> HENRY STEELE COMMAGER

Without a plan, you will risk falling into gender-based traditional roles, especially if you have children. When you and your partner make a plan for accomplishing household tasks and parenting responsibilities, do not focus on gender as a construct of differences between men and women. Learn from happy couples and base decisions on personal preferences instead. The idea that some characteristics are always "male" and some are always "female" is often just stereotyping. In many cases, there are fathers who have more patience and nurturance for small children than do their wives. Is it wrong to let these dads lead in the role of parenting responsibility? Gender stereotypes do not reflect individuality and are often inaccurate. Worse, these differences are often used to legitimize and perpetuate power relations between men and women.

The first step to formulating a plan is documenting what the current household and childrearing chores are and who has taken responsibility for them. In preparation for this, and for the role-reversal exercise later, write down the tasks you each complete on a daily or weekly basis that are related to the household and (if applicable) the children. Make sure to include all the tasks, actions, arrangements, and so on. This is often difficult, because many of the household management tasks are executed as they occur. Nonetheless, do the best you can to write down not only the physical tasks (e.g., walk the dog, drive child to piano lesson) but also the more mental responsibilities that are kept in your head (e.g., make sure dog does not dig in the garden, remind child to practice piano). If possible, add to your list over a course of several days, or even a week, in order to get a more accurate account of your responsibilities.

Once your lists are completed, sit down with your partner to have a conversation about your lists and the feelings surrounding your responsibilities contained in these lists. Discuss the following questions in your dialogue: Who did this task in your family of origin (the family you grew up in)? Who did you expect would do this task before you were married? Who took care of this task when you were first married? Rate how you feel about this task on a scale of 1 to 10. How much time does this task consume for you on a weekly basis? How would you feel if this task were no longer your responsibility?

Expect to learn a lot from this discussion. You may even decide to divide a task your partner enjoys for the overall benefit of the family. Remember Cindy and Vin's decision to share the job of cooking dinner? Vin loves to cook but was spending a disproportionate amount of time on this one task. Cindy and Vin decided that sharing and simplifying dinner allowed them more precious family time together to do other things.

Be Creative and Flexible

Expand your thinking as much as possible as you go through the process of redistributing roles. Hire outside help if you desire (and can afford to). Share jobs neither of you enjoy. This can be done together or by alternating responsibility. Create a chore chart and post it in a visible spot. If you have children, set up a structure of sharing when it comes to being the primary on-call parent for day care or schools.

Be open to changing responsibilities through time and situations. It has been said that the most successful people are those who are good at plan B. Once you find a situation in which you and your partner are happy, keep in mind that this will not always be the way it is. If you have children, they will be given new household responsibilities as they grow, so chores will need to be redistributed periodically. Then, as the children grow up and leave the home, they will need to be revised once more. Happy couples have a continued capacity for growth and change, as change is the one constant of life.

CHECK-IN PROCESS

Where are you *now*? (Identify and discuss your results.)

1. Review the Couple Checkup *individual* results. How satisfied were each of you in this area?

_____

_____

2. Review the Couple Checkup *couple* results. Was "roles" a strength or growth area?

_____

_____

3. Discuss your agreement items (your strengths).

_____

_____

Where would you like to be? (Discuss issues.)

1. Review the discussion items in your Couple Checkup report.

2. Choose one issue you both want to resolve.

3. Share how you each feel about the issue.

How do you get there? (Develop your action plan.)

1. Brainstorm a list of ways to handle your role problems.

2. Agree on one solution you will try.

3. Decide what you will each do to make the plan work.

4. Review the progress in one week.

COUPLE EXERCISE 7.1
Household Tasks: His and Hers

1. List your responsibilities related to the household and the children. Make a list of daily responsibilities (e.g., planning and preparing meals, walking the dog, helping child with homework) and weekly responsibilities (e.g., doing yard work, taking out recycling, washing a floor). Your partner should also separately create the same two lists.

Things You Do Daily	Things You Do Weekly
1. _____	1. _____
2. _____	2. _____
3. _____	3. _____
4. _____	4. _____
5. _____	5. _____
6. _____	6. _____
7. _____	7. _____
8. _____	8. _____
9. _____	9. _____
10. _____	10. _____

2. After you have each completed your lists, compare and discuss them. Focus on what you each would like to change about who handles which household tasks.

3. Revise your current lists, finalizing an agreement about tasks you will each do next week. Set a time to review the new lists.

COUPLE EXERCISE 7.2
Switching Roles for One Week

After you have each completed Exercise 7.1, plan a day (or preferably a week) when you can perform each other's household responsibilities. This role-reversal experiment will help you gain a new appreciation for one another.

REMINDERS FOR IMPROVING THE QUALITY OF YOUR ROLE RELATIONSHIP

1. Remove gender from housework. Talk about and divide housework based on interests and skills rather than on gender.

2. Work to develop and maintain an equal relationship in terms of power and decision making.

3. Keep an ongoing discussion of your expectations and feelings regarding roles and changes you would like to make.

4. Working together on tasks works best for most couples.

5. Take a good look at how your work schedules may contribute to inequality at home.

6. Express appreciation to your partner for the contributions he or she makes to your family and home life.

7. Be flexible and open to change.

EIGHT

SPIRITUALITY— LIVE OUT YOUR VALUES

*We are not human beings having a spiritual experience;
we are spiritual beings having a human experience.*

—PIERRE TEILHARD DE CHARDIN

Why is there suffering in the world? What is the meaning of life? What happens before birth and after death? These are just a few of life's questions where science and rational thought are inadequate to provide answers. These questions call to our spirit or subjective mind, and people have always looked to religion or spirituality to make sense of these seemingly inexplicable questions.

Spirituality and faith are powerful and prevalent dimensions of the human experience. According to anthropologists, nearly every culture on earth contains at least one religion that shares certain supernatural features, including belief in a God or gods, belief in life after death, and belief in the ability of prayer or ritual to change the course of human events. In America, 70 percent of people claim membership in a church or synagogue, with nearly 90 percent of all adults indicating that religion is important in their lives.[1]

Membership in organized religion is the common way to practice one's faith and grow spiritually. But for many in our current culture, participation in organized religion is not recognized as a requirement, nor is it necessarily an indicator of a person's spirituality. We recommend, however, that people worship and grow their faith within a community of believers as this provides a great source of strength and encouragement throughout the seasons of life. Couples, for example, can meet with a small group of other couples or be mentored by an older, more experienced couple to study this book and apply the principles to their relationships. Doing so helps to bring the principles of this research to life in a very personal way. But our spirit is also nurtured by the discipline of solitude. According to Mother Teresa,

> We need to find God, and he cannot be found in noise and restlessness. God is the friend of silence. See how nature—trees, flowers, grass—grows in silence; see the stars, the moon and the sun, how they move in silence . . . We need silence to be able to touch souls.[2]

A distinction between religion and spirituality is often understood. Spirituality describes a multifaceted relationship between human and metaphysical systems, whereas religion is used more often to describe specific doctrines or beliefs within the metaphysical realm. For the purpose of this chapter and in harmony with the Couple Checkup items, "spirituality" and "religious beliefs" are used interchangeably to describe the multifaceted connection between an individual and her spiritual beliefs and practices.

Spirituality is deeply personal, as we come to our own faith journey through a combination of our upbringing, our education, our beliefs, and ultimately, our own encounter with the divine. A person's belief system represents his or her view of reality. And a marriage naturally unites two people with their own value and belief systems.

Globalization has increased our exposure to different religions and spiritual practices, often putting a face on the religious variety and complexity that may have once seemed foreign to us. Interfaith marriages are more common than ever before. This religious pluralism has the potential to become either a divisive force or one to unify, depending on how it is approached. One study of interfaith marriages found that happy couples deemphasize their spiritual differences and emphasize the similarities, while couples who emphasize theological differences have lingering conflicts.[3]

BENEFITS OF FAITH

Past research has disputed whether or not a connection exists between spirituality and quality of marriage. Some studies report small ties between religiosity and decreased probability of divorce,[4] but other research suggests that an increase in religious activity has little relation to better-quality marriages.[5]

More recent research has documented the benefits of faith and congregational support on individual well-being.[6] There is also evidence of the positive role religion plays in marriage and for adolescents.[7] A recent study found that couples who integrate religion into their marriages have less marital conflict, more verbal collaboration, greater marital adjustment, and more perceived benefits from marriage. Studies have linked a higher level of parental religiosity with a variety of positive outcomes for teens, including less behavior problems, higher GPAs, more satisfaction with their families, and more volunteerism and civic participation.[8]

Agreement on spiritual beliefs in couples seems to be related to them having strengths in other areas of their marriages. A study by authors Peter Larson and David Olson of over twelve thousand married couples compared those who had high agreement on spiritual beliefs with those having low agreement. Couples who had high spiritual agreement reported much higher levels of satisfaction in most other important areas of their relationships (see Figure 8.1). Those with high agreement had greater marital satisfaction and felt better about their communication and conflict resolution, financial management, sexual relationship, closeness, and flexibility as a couple.[9]

> "Without faith, nothing is possible. With it, nothing is impossible."
>
> MARY MCLEOD BETHUNE

SPIRITUAL STRENGTHS OF HAPPY COUPLES

The majority of happy couples we studied had several spiritual strengths that strengthen their bond and add meaning to all facets of their life.

FIGURE 8.1
High vs. Low Spirituality Agreement

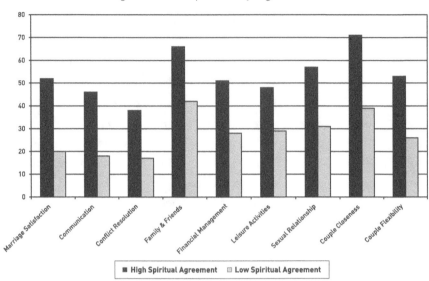

Beliefs That Provide Meaning to Life

Many people say their faith is part of a personal mission upon which they base their actions. For them, religion provides a context and perspective that keeps them focused on long-term goals rather than short-term gratification. Their beliefs guide their daily actions with regard to morality, integrity, relationships, love, finances, and more.

A shared spiritual relationship can provide a significant foundation for a growing marital relationship. In a real sense, God's unconditional love is a model for partnership. A couple's mutual faith helps them focus on the positive aspects of each other and encourage and respect one another. Their marriage is a sanctuary—a source of care, mutual protection, comfort, and refuge. While feelings can often vacillate, their faith provides the foundation for a commitment that sustains the relationship.

FIGURE 8.2
Strengths of Happy Couples vs. Unhappy Couples
Regarding Spirituality

Spiritual Issue	Percentage in Agreement	
	Happy Couples	Unhappy Couples
1. I am satisfied with how we express our spiritual values and beliefs.	85%	40%
2. I feel closer to my spouse because of shared spiritual beliefs.	78%	43%
3. Sharing spiritual beliefs strengthens our relationship.	83%	50%
4. Spiritual differences do not cause tension in our relationship.	86%	56%
5. We rely on our spiritual beliefs during difficult times.	77%	46%

Satisfaction with Spiritual Expression

In our national survey, the key factor that distinguished happy couples from unhappy ones in terms of religion was agreement on their level of satisfaction with how spiritual values and beliefs are expressed. Most happily married couples (85 percent) agree on this item, compared with only 40 percent of unhappily married couples.

In his twenty-five-plus years as a trial court judge and in his study of biblical principles, Judge James Sheridan claims to have never seen a divorce involving a couple whose lives truly expressed the biblical model of marriage. He contends, "Indeed couples that follow God's model are happily married and enjoy a truly passionate and intimate sex and romance life."[10]

Expression of spiritual beliefs can be thought of on two different levels: shared through communication or lived through expression. The communication level is more straightforward: through language and nonverbal communication we share our beliefs with our partners. The next level relates to Judge James Sheridan's observation—that our lives become a living expression of God's plan. A solid agreement on these two levels appears to be most successful for couples.

Feeling Closer Because of Shared Beliefs

Often spiritual beliefs are practiced individually and not integrated into a couple relationship. Although spirituality can also be regarded as a private matter, we know that shared religious faith can strengthen a marriage. Figure 8.2 summarizes our findings on happily married and unhappily married couples. Happily married couples are much more likely to agree (78 percent) that they feel closer as a couple because of their spiritual beliefs than unhappily married couples are (43 percent).

If you consider yourself secular, this does not mean you do not or cannot share a spiritual connection with your partner. Human beings are more than the sum of our atoms. Even "pure" science recognizes the existence of forces beyond matter, demonstrated by the placebo effect often observed when testing new drugs and medical treatments. Religion, with its mind-focused teachings, rituals, and beliefs, has been described as "from the outside in," while spirituality, with its experiential focus has been described as "from the inside out."[11] The following "from the inside out" questions touch on the human experience that logic cannot always address. Whether or not you are identified with a particular religion, which may or may not inform these answers, spend some time with your partner sharing your responses to these questions. You may find them to illuminate the complexity and frailty of life while they engage you and your partner to live intentionally and thoughtfully.

- What matters in life?
- Describe the first time you remember being aware of your bodily mortality.

- Is life an accident?

- What virtue would you give to all human beings?

- When do you feel most at peace with yourself?

- How has your understanding of God changed through your life?

- Describe the most spiritual person you have ever met.

- What do you believe happens after death?

- Describe a time when you felt the influence of divine grace.

- What is the meaning of life?

- When do your personal values and actions intersect?

Freedom to Share Beliefs

Like sex and money, spiritual beliefs are often difficult for couples to talk about. The fact is that relationships are generally linguistic systems in nature. They begin and persist through the process of language between people. It is only through communication about beliefs, even if they are not similar, where understanding and loving become possible.

Eighty-three percent of happily married couples agree that sharing their spiritual beliefs helps their relationship stay strong. This is a testament to the power of communication. Don Miguel Ruiz, in his book *The Four Agreements*, describes the power of language:

> The word is not just a sound or a written symbol. The word is a force; it is the power you have to express and communicate, to think, and thereby to create the events in your life. Your word is the power you have to create. Your word is the gift that comes directly from God. Through the word you express your creative power. It is through the word that you manifest everything regardless of what language you speak.[12]

Be continuously curious about your partner's spiritual beliefs. Remember everything is alive and changing all the time, so you cannot assume their beliefs have remained stagnant and unchanged. Faith is a lifelong journey. It is as simple as beginning a conversation; conversation leads to confession, and confession unifies and strengthens your partnership.

Mary and Dale are a couple who, after five years of marriage, were surprised to discover their different preferences for their children's education were related to their spiritual beliefs. During a dinner party conversation, the discussion turned to private Christian education versus public education. Mary voiced loud support for public education. Although they had never had this discussion as a couple, Dale assumed their membership and participation at church would inform her decision to send their children to the private school sponsored by their church. As they drove home from the dinner party, they could have engaged in heated debate and argued their various points. Instead of focusing on different positions, Dale used language to their advantage by focusing on questions, which are shared, rather than on answers, which divide.

By stating, "Honey, I know we both want the best for the kids, so help me understand your thoughts and feelings about our school options." Dale opened the door for a new kind of conversation. This new direction engenders compassion, a core virtue in every spiritual tradition. It also helps avoid judgment, replacing it with curiosity and a desire to understand. Krista Tippett, in her book *Speaking of Faith*, observes that faith is as much about questions as it is about certainties. She says, "It is possible to be a believer and a listener at the same time, to be both fervent and searching, to nurture a vital identity and to wonder at the identities of others."[13]

TENSION IN YOUR RELATIONSHIP CAUSED BY SPIRITUAL DIFFERENCES

If you are a couple whose differences in spiritual beliefs cause tension in your relationship, you are much more similar to unhappy couples in this dimension of your marriage. When differences come up, remember that faith, by its very nature, cannot always be rationalized or explained. Be wary of religious certainty, especially when it is used to discard other viewpoints or spread hatred and judgment. Remember, Jesus handed out perhaps his harshest criticism to the religious leaders of his day who were certain they were fulfilling God's law to perfect standards.

All one needs to do is to remember the horrors inflicted on humanity in the name of religious certainty to see the danger and potential corruption this mind-set can have. The type of political power that Christianity exerted during the Crusades or the Inquisition, for instance, can today be observed in some of the fundamental varieties of Islam. So, when you become judgmental and intolerant of other faith practices, especially your partner's, you must remember that the religion you affiliate with is an imperfect institution practiced by imperfect people. Even moral libertarians and secular analysts claim to be repelled by the intolerance and absoluteness of religion, while failing to recognize that they may be practicing the same intolerance they abhor.

> "Faith is an act of a finite being who is grasped by, and turned to, the infinite."
>
> PAUL TILLICH

Mother Teresa, a nun who dedicated her life to serving the poor of the largely Hindu nation India, once said, "Let no one ever come to you without leaving better and happier. Be the living expression of God's kindness: kindness in your face, kindness in your eyes, kindness in your smile."[14] Can you practice God's kindness with a partner who holds different beliefs? Instead of getting into a battle of attacking and defending beliefs, find ways to honor and respect your partner even as you discuss differing beliefs. Use the questions at the end of the chapter to create this discourse, and take advantage of the spiritual realm to enrich and nourish your couple relationship instead of dividing and diminishing it. The keys to these different outcomes are good communication skills (see chapter 3), focusing on similarities, and understanding differences. Martin Luther King Jr. revealed a powerful perspective in statements such as, "I have decided to stick with love. Hate is too great a burden to bear."[15]

A REFUGE IN TIMES OF CRISIS

We can learn from happy couples to rely on our faith during difficult times—they turn to faith much more frequently than unhappy couples do. We all experience difficult times—no one is immune to sadness, loss, or grief; it is part of the package of life. Sometimes faith and prayer are the only arsenal against events that make no sense.

The Bible teaches that suffering is normal and makes us stronger. In spite of suffering, when it would appear as though God is absent, God is always present. God's timing is perfect, and it is important to keep faith and trust in God during times of suffering. Luke 24:13–35 tells the story of how two of Jesus' disciples were returning from Jerusalem, upset after witnessing the crucifixion of their Lord. It was the third day, and they were discouraged that Jesus had not risen from the dead as he had promised. They had started walking back home, perhaps having given up faith, when "Jesus himself came up and walked along with them" (v. 15 NIV). They were unaware that Jesus had been walking next to them the whole time.

In Buddhism, suffering or dissatisfaction is recognized as one of the three basic principles of human existence. Acknowledging the presence of suffering is not intended to convey a negative worldview but rather a pragmatic approach. Suffering is caused by desire and ignorance; desire being a craving for pleasure, material goods, and immortality; ignorance being not understanding our attachment to these impermanent things. Because all we crave is transient, their loss, and therefore our suffering, is inevitable. Buddhism teaches the end of suffering through a sophisticated process involving ethical and mental development, but the cause of suffering must first be recognized before this process can begin.

Relying on faith during difficult times allows us to experience dissatisfaction without shutting down relationally. One way to practice this is by extending compassion and kindness to others and also inwardly. Remember, faith is not a commodity we either possess or do not possess. Faith is a verb; it is something we do. And reaching out to God and others during difficult times is a way we access faith. Faith and prayer can be a great resource during difficult times in your couple relationship, as well as being building blocks to intimacy.

COMMON SPIRITUALITY ISSUES FOR COUPLES

The most common challenges for couples in terms of spiritual beliefs, according to our national survey of fifty thousand couples, are summarized in Figure 8.3. Compared to other relationship issues, spiritual beliefs have a lower overall disagreement rate among married couples.

FIGURE 8.3
Top Five Issues Regarding Spiritual Beliefs

Issue	Percentage of Couples Having Problem*
1. We have not resolved the differences in our spiritual beliefs.	52%
2. We do not feel closer as a result of our spiritual beliefs.	47%
3. We do not rely on our spiritual beliefs during difficult times.	45%
4. We are dissatisfied with how we express our spiritual values and beliefs.	45%
5. Spiritual differences cause tension in our relationship.	34%

One or both partners indicated this was an issue for them.

Differences in Spiritual Beliefs

The most common spiritual issue for all couples in our survey was unresolved differences in their spiritual beliefs, with 52 percent of all couples having this problem. These findings are important, as spiritual beliefs provide a foundation for the values and behaviors of individuals and couples. Given the potential benefits of spiritual beliefs in a relationship, it makes sense for partners to explore and evaluate their compatibility regarding spiritual beliefs. Couples with strong spiritual beliefs and practices say their faith provides a foundation that deepens their love and helps them grow together and achieve their dreams. Even if partners hold dissimilar views, they can still have a committed, strong spiritual life that adds meaning and purpose to their existence. The following couple had difficulty knowing how to handle their differences in spiritual beliefs.

Cal and Jennifer were young when they fell in love. They were both just twenty years old when they married, and their parents expressed concern. Cal was raised in a traditional Catholic family. Jennifer grew up in a Jewish family. When they were young, these differences didn't seem a big deal. Neither of them were very involved in their own religious practices. Religion felt more like something handed down from their parents, not a personal priority. For several years they were happy to move forward in their marriage relatively removed from any church or religious association.

Things began to change a few years later when Cal's father passed away. Losing his dad was very difficult for Cal, and he began to meet with a priest to receive counsel and comfort through a local church. Soon, he felt a renewed commitment to the church and his Catholic faith. About that same time, Jennifer gave birth to their first child, and they began to question how they would raise their son. Cal expressed an interest in Catholic school. Jennifer wished he would get over his newfound "churchy" phase. She was not on board with sending their child to be "indoctrinated" into Cal's belief system. What had been a nonissue for many years now reared its head as the biggest challenge facing their marriage.

Not Feeling Closer

Forty-seven percent of our surveyed married couples do not feel any closer to each other because of their spiritual beliefs. It is unclear from this finding alone whether or not these couples had high or low spiritual compatibility. For couples who don't identify with a specific religion or faith practice, they rarely connect on a spiritual level. Many who do participate in organized religion choose to not talk about or share their personal spiritual life with their partners, almost compartmentalizing their spiritual experiences as something they do and practice only at the church, synagogue, or mosque.

For other couples, their faith practices and spiritual beliefs are the very things that draw them toward one another. Many couples choose to learn, pray, and worship together on a regular basis. Some build a strong community of faith and support around their marriage and family through participating in a church, mosque, or synagogue. Retreats, classes, and family activities are embraced, integrating spirituality into all aspects of their life. For these couples, their faith tends to draw them nearer to one another.

Not Relying on Spiritual Beliefs During Difficult Times

While half of all couples do rely on their spiritual beliefs during difficult times, nearly half (45 percent) report they do not. But difficult times can occur very quickly. You may be enjoying financial freedom when suddenly your job is cut because the company you work for experiences problems. Or you are happily settled into your life when a family member becomes seriously ill. Spiritual beliefs give us resiliency in a life we cannot always control. This resiliency can provide peace and inner strength no matter what our circumstances may be. As Martin Luther King Jr. said, "We must accept finite disappointment, but never lose infinite hope."[16]

Dissatisfied with How You Express Spiritual Beliefs and Values

Couples often have different desires and values with regard to how they want to express their faith. One partner may value regular attendance at a place of worship, while another may feel that spirituality is not linked to this practice. Melanie and Davis are a couple who experienced problems when it came to expressing their faith. They met and were married in a Christian church. Melanie became active in community outreach to the poor and social justice issues, which she enjoys and feels fulfills the teachings of Jesus to help others and create a more just society. Davis is certainly not opposed to these activities, but he believes they are of little value unless she is also spreading the Word of God. Melanie has begun to feel irritated at what she feels is Davis's rigid ideas about church doctrine and his insistence that reaching out to others must always include proselytizing.

Like all couples, Melanie and Davis face both challenges and opportunities when it comes to their spiritual beliefs. They can stand against one another with a critical and judgmental spirit that fosters conflict and division, or they can approach their differences with a spirit of love that fosters understanding and connection in their marriage.

CHECK-IN PROCESS

Where are you *now*? (Identify and discuss your results.)

1. Review the Couple Checkup *individual* results. How satisfied were each of you in this area?

_____

_____

2. Review the Couple Checkup *couple* results. Was spirituality a strength or growth area?

_____

_____

3. Discuss your agreement items (your strengths).

_____

_____

Where would you like to be? (Discuss issues.)

1. Review the discussion items in your Couple Checkup report.

2. Choose one issue you both want to resolve.

3. Share how you each feel about the issue.

How do you get there? (Develop your action plan.)

1. Brainstorm a list of ways to handle your spirituality problems.

2. Agree on one solution you will try.

3. Decide what you will each do to make the plan work.

4. Review the progress in one week.

COUPLE EXERCISE 8.1
Exploring Your Past

How much do you know about your partner's religious history? How much do you know about your own religious history? Family heritage lends a sense of stability and tranquility to relationships.

Set aside some time to discuss the following questions. If you do not have the answers, ask other family members or contact a historical society.

1. What is your family's ethnicity?
2. What is the origin of your family name? (In biblical times, names often were connected to race or profession.)
3. What is your family's religion?
4. What holidays (holy days) and rituals do you and your partner currently celebrate?
5. Where did those celebrations originate?
6. What do holiday symbols mean, like the menorah and Christmas tree?
7. Is there significance to the food you prepare?
8. What is the meaning of the gifts you exchange?

Through rituals, we create a treasure chest of memories, communicate information about values, and build a family legacy for our children and grandchildren. With that in mind, create a new family or couple ritual. Then integrate it into your weekly, monthly, or yearly routines.

COUPLE EXERCISE 8.2
Celebrating the Small Stuff

Set aside a quiet time to sit down with your partner. Try one of the following exercises:

1. **Write down three uplifting moments in which you felt energized during the last month.** Picture those moments when you felt most alive—when the commonplace became not so

common—such as the slant of late winter rays of sunlight, good work well done, a game of touch football in the fall leaves, or rocking your child to sleep. Share your experiences with each other.

2. **Write down the names of the three people with whom you are most joyful.** Then write down the names of the three people who you trust the most. Share the names on both lists with your partner. Talk about why you trust the people you named. Discuss specific reasons you enjoy the people you named.

REMINDERS FOR IMPROVING SPIRITUALITY IN YOUR RELATIONSHIP

1. Take time to learn about your partner's view of spirituality.
2. Integrate aspects of your spiritual lives into your couple relationship.
3. Establish rituals that will honor your spiritual beliefs.
4. Access faith by connecting with God, your partner, and others during difficult times.
5. Consider ways you could pray or worship together as a couple.

NINE

CLOSENESS AND FLEXIBILITY— MAP YOUR RELATIONSHIP

In your couple relationship, you either repeat what you learned in your family or you tend to do the opposite.

—DAVID H. OLSON

CLOSENESS AND FLEXIBILITY— KEYS TO A GREAT MARRIAGE

One of the major discoveries in our national survey was the importance of couple closeness and couple flexibility in happy marriages. Past studies have continually found that communication and conflict resolution are what most distinguished happy from unhappy couples, but in our survey, closeness and flexibility were found to be as important as communication and conflict resolution when predicting marital success.

This new discovery about closeness and flexibility is understandable when you consider our fast-paced and highly stressed society in which partners often spend time away from each other at their jobs, in their cars, or shuttling kids to activities. Closeness is a powerful predictor because happy couples have learned not only how to do their own thing but how to reconnect with each other. Our fast-paced lives require a greater need to be flexible and open to change. Roles that are not clearly defined, such as who will leave work to pick up a sick child, need to be negotiated. Flexibility helps couples adapt to challenges today and thereby maintain a happy marriage.

THE COUPLE AND FAMILY MAP

The Couple and Family Map is based on two key relational dimensions: closeness and flexibility. The Couple Map will help you better understand both your couple relationship and family of origin. It will also enable you to see the linkage between the two, which otherwise may not be so obvious. The Couple and Family Map identifies twenty-five different styles of relationships. Based on your results from the Couple Checkup or the Couple Quiz (at the end of this chapter), you can plot how you perceive your relationship on the Couple Map.

CLOSENESS

Closeness describes how emotionally connected you feel to your partner or other family members. It describes your ability to balance separateness and togetherness—your private space and your intimate connection. The Couple and Family Map breaks closeness down into five levels, from disconnected at the lowest level, to connected in the middle, to overly connected on the high end. Figure 9.1 describes the five levels of closeness: the three central levels considered "balanced" on separateness and togetherness, and the high and low levels "unbalanced," as they represent too much or too little closeness.

Finding the right balance between separateness and togetherness is the key to healthy couple and family closeness. Although being disconnected (too much separateness) or overly connected (too much togetherness) can be appropriate at times, relationships that most often operate at these extremes tend to be unhealthy—the lack of balance creates problems. Finding a balance that is right for you and your partner between these extremes is what leads to greatest couple happiness.

It is normal for couple and family relationships to shift back and forth between togetherness and separateness depending on what is happening in the relationship. But couples and families that get locked into an unbalanced level of closeness (too much or too little) tend to have more problems than those who don't.

FIGURE 9.1

Five Levels of Closeness, Balancing Separateness vs. Togetherness

	Separateness vs. Togetherness	
Disconnected System		**Unbalanced** *high separateness*
Somewhat Connected System		**Balanced** *more separateness than togetherness*
Connected System		**Balanced** *equal separateness and togetherness*
Very Connected System		**Balanced** *more togetherness than separateness*
Overly Connected System		**Unbalanced** *very high togetherness*

The level of closeness experienced in your couple and family relationships comes to life when in real interactions such as mealtimes, birthdays, or celebrating holidays.

Take, for example, Lori and Tim, a married couple. In Lori's family everyone was expected to be present at dinnertime. They used this time for family members to socialize and reconnect with one another. Lori has many fond memories of shared dinners—laughing, talking, and discussing family issues during this important time.

In contrast, Tim's family did not place much importance on shared mealtimes. Since his was a large family with six kids and each individual had a different schedule, family members ate their dinner whenever they pleased. It was even common for family members to grab a plate of food and watch TV or retreat to their bedrooms.

Not surprisingly, Tim and Lori's different experiences and values about dinnertime affected their closeness and initially caused some problems in their marriage. Lori expected that she and Tim would be together during dinner to talk about their day and what was coming up for each of them. For Tim, dinnertime was not a priority. He wondered why Lori seemed so withdrawn if he stayed late at the office or decided to go out with his teammates after their company softball games. And he couldn't understand why Lori got so upset if he watched television while he ate.

This is a fairly nonthreatening example of how closeness is reflected in everyday interactions. Still, it is not uncommon for little issues, like dinnertime rituals, to erode the quality of a couple's closeness and feelings of connection. It is important to be aware that we often repeat the styles we learn from our families of origin, where our expectations for closeness are often formed. Also, keep in mind that good communication is the facilitating factor for negotiating and making changes in the closeness of your relationship.

Balancing Separateness and Togetherness

Couples and families that maintain a happy, healthy relationship strike a good balance between spending time together and spending time separately. In these couples and families, each member develops both dependence on the family and also independence of his or her own. This kind of balance is a comfortable one in which members can move back and forth between separateness and togetherness with ease. Of course, sometimes things will get out of balance, and that's OK—as long as you do not get stuck there.

Kahlil Gibran describes a balance between separateness and togetherness in his poem "On Marriage":

> Sing and dance together and be joyous, but let each one of you be alone,
> Even as the strings of a lute are alone though they quiver with the same music.
> Give your hearts, but not into each other's keeping.
> For only the hand of Life can contain your hearts.
> And stand together yet not too near together:
> For the pillars of the temple stand apart,
> And the oak tree and the cypress grow not in each other's shadow.
> But let there be spaces in your togetherness,
> And let the winds of the heavens dance between you.[1]

The relationship Gibran describes is an ideal balance between separateness and togetherness. Finding this kind of balance takes time, hard work, and commitment. In cohesive relationships individuals place emphasis on self as well as the couple. They strive for an appropriate amount of sharing, loyalty, intimacy, and independence. These couples make room for individual interests and shared activities. They can take occasional trips with just the guys or girls as well as vacation as a couple. They each know how to care for themselves as well as invest in the other person's needs. They learn how to balance their development as individuals with the growth of the relationship. Successful couples and families tend to be those that have achieved an appropriate balance between the individual and couple. Partners maintain their own individuality *and* their closeness.

FIGURE 9.2

Strengths of Happy Couples versus
Unhappy Couples on Couple Closeness

Closeness Issue	Percentage in Agreement	
	Happy Couples	Unhappy Couples
1. We feel very close to each other.	93%	29%
2. Our togetherness is a top priority for us.	83%	30%
3. We really enjoy spending our free time together.	95%	45%
4. We ask each other for help.	92%	43%
5. We find it easy to think of things to do together.	81%	30%

When happy couples were compared with unhappy couples in our national survey, there were distinct differences between the two samples in couple closeness. Figure 9.2 summarizes the key findings. Almost all (93 percent) of the happy couples agree that both partners feel very close to one another, whereas only 29 percent of unhappy couples feel that way. Most happy couples describe togetherness as a top priority, but less than a third (30 percent) of unhappy couples agree with that idea. Partners in happy marriages are more than twice as likely as unhappy couples to find it easy to think of things to do together, enjoy doing things together, and they ask each other for help.

Avoiding Extreme Separateness or Closeness

Figure 9.1 depicts five levels of couple and family closeness. Having a very low or a very high level of closeness can eventually lead to problems. When a relationship is "disconnected"—not close—the individuals tend to focus more on themselves than on each other. They may have too much separateness and be highly independent. They may feel that they cannot count on their relationship to give them support when they need it. Fritz Perls expresses the idea of extreme separateness in the "Gestalt Prayer":

I do my thing and you do your thing.
I am not in this world to live up to your expectations,
And you are not in this world to live up to mine.
You are you and I am I, and if by chance we find each other, it's beautiful.
If not, it can't be helped.[2]

The polar opposite—"overly connected" relationships, with an extreme amount of closeness—is not ideal either. In these relationships members can have too much togetherness, demand loyalty, become too dependent on one another, and have little private time or space. In overly connected relationships, the needs of the relationship often come before the needs of the individuals. Judy Altura expresses extreme closeness in her "Togetherness Poem":

We do everything together.
I am here to meet all your needs and expectations.
And you are here to meet mine.
We had to meet, and it was beautiful.
I can't imagine it turning out any other way.[3]

FLEXIBILITY

Flexibility refers to how open to change couples and families are in their relationships. Flexibility describes the amount of change that occurs, for example, in leadership, role relationships, and relationship rules. As with closeness, there are five levels of flexibility, from "inflexible" on the low end, to "flexible" in the middle, to "overly flexible" on the high end. Again, the two extremes can work within relationships in the short run, but over time they are unhealthy. The flexibility component on the Couple and Family Map assesses how the couple or family system balances stability and change (see Figure 9.3).

FIGURE 9.3
Five Levels of Flexibility, Balancing Stability, & Change

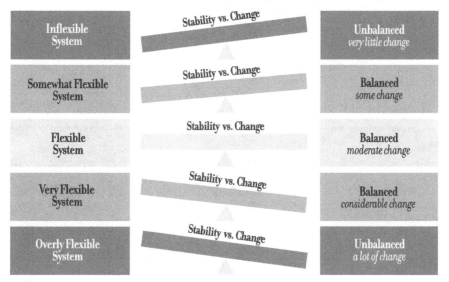

Balancing Stability and Change

Balancing the amount of stability versus change in your couple and family relationships is increasingly important as lives get busy. Since change is inevitable, relationships must be open to it and able to find the right balance for both partners. But relationships also want and need stability. Without stability, couples cannot meet the demands of daily living or functioning in our fast-paced society. They need to know who will pay the bills this month, who will attend their child's parent-teacher conference, and who will do the laundry this week.

Relationships that have "balanced" levels of flexibility are somewhat structured, and members sometimes share leadership. Roles are well defined and stable, but they can change depending on current needs. Flexibility becomes vital in times of crisis as members adapt to changing conditions and roles while coping with stress. Relationships that function well at these times are still considered balanced because they operate in one of the extremes for only a short period of time before returning to a more equal state.

When happy and unhappy couples' relationship flexibility was compared, some clear differences emerged on important aspects of their relationship (see Figure 9.4). For instance, happy couples agree more often than unhappy ones to compromise and make decisions jointly. Happy couples also are better able to adjust to change, are more creative in handling conflict, and more often share leadership. In many ways, happy couples work together more as a team and cooperate rather than compete with each other.

FIGURE 9.4
Strengths of Happy Couples versus Unhappy Couples on Flexibility

Flexibility Issue	Percentage in Agreement	
	Happy Couples	Unhappy Couples
1. We compromise when problems arise.	83%	28%
2. We make most decisions jointly.	91%	42%
3. Both of us are able to adjust to change when it's necessary.	85%	35%

4. We are creative in how we handle our differences.	**58%**	**14%**
5. We share leadership equally.	**63%**	**23%**

Avoiding Extreme Stability or Change

Figure 9.3 depicts five levels of family flexibility. Couples and families with very low levels of flexibility are described as "inflexible." In an inflexible relationship, rules rarely change, even to accommodate special situations or adjust to life changes. In these relationships people rarely negotiate; roles are very stable. For families, discipline is strict and often characterized by authoritarian leadership.

Kyle and Judy were two very structured and organized individuals. They had both done advanced graduate work and were quite successful in their careers. When it came to their marriage and household, they ran a tight ship. There was always a to-do list hanging in the kitchen, and they stuck to a predictable schedule and routine.

Things began to change after they had twin girls. When the kids were young, the routines and structure worked very well for keeping up with twins. But Kyle and Judy failed to increase flexibility as their girls became teenagers. Holding to the same strict rules that had been set when the kids were much younger, they had little tolerance for the shifts that were taking place. Their girls were expressing their natural need for more freedom and choices in their lives. When one of their daughters broke curfew or questioned the rules, Kyle and Judy's natural tendency was to become even stricter, trying to get the girls back in line. Before long, they had two rebellious, angry teenage girls on their hands. When everything else in their lives seemed to work so well, Kyle and Judy were confused about their inability to be effective parents to teenagers.

At the other extreme are "overly flexible" relationships, which have too much change. In overly flexible relationships, there is often so much change that these couples or families function almost completely without structure, roles, or rules. Excessive change is disruptive and leads to feelings of insecurity within the family. When rules and roles frequently change, things do not get done, and the lack of order limits productivity within the family. Overly flexible relationships are off balance and feel chaotic because of so much change.

COMMON ISSUES RELATED TO CLOSENESS AND FLEXIBILITY

A common problem for couples coming for counseling is that they disagree on how much closeness or flexibility they want in their relationship. For example, one person might want to spend more time together while the other wants more freedom and autonomy. Couples might also differ on how organized they should be, as one person prefers an unscheduled weekend while the other likes to have activities organized and planned.

Another issue for couples is that they are stuck on the unbalanced extremes of closeness or flexibility. A common complaint of couples seeking counseling is that there is too little closeness (i.e., too much separateness) between them because they have drifted apart as they each are more involved in work or activities away from their partner. Another common complaint is that their partner is too rigid and is not open to change (i.e., inflexible).

An important step in creating a relationship that will work for both of you is to take the Couple Checkup and discover how you each perceive your relationship. One common finding is that partners see their relationship somewhat differently in terms of closeness and flexibility. Another important step is to consider how much closeness and flexibility you would each like to have in your relationship. By comparing where you are now to where you would like to be, you can begin to set goals to change your relationship and explore how you might achieve these goals together.

BALANCED, MIDRANGE, AND UNBALANCED COUPLES

In the Couple Map (see Figure 9.5), the five levels of closeness and the five levels of flexibility are combined, and together they create twenty-five different types of couple relationships. These twenty-five types can be broken down into three more general patterns (balanced, midrange, and unbalanced).

FIGURE 9.5

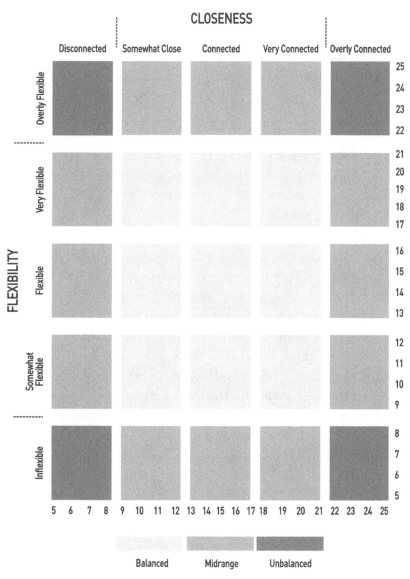

The nine central cells (lightly shaded) are called "balanced" because they are the three central levels of both closeness and flexibility. Couples in a balanced relationship are typically the most happy.

There are twelve "midrange" types (medium-shaded cells), which occur when a couple is balanced in one area and unbalanced in the other. These couples can be happy and be doing well, but they often have more difficulty when they encounter stress in their lives.

There are four "unbalanced" types (darkest shaded cells). These represent a couple at the extremes of both closeness and flexibility. Couples who are unbalanced typically are not very happy with the relationship and are most likely to seek counseling for their marriage. A more balanced approach to closeness and flexibility is best for relationships as they grow and change over time.

DYNAMIC BALANCE AND SKIING

Achieving a balanced relationship in both closeness and flexibility is not an easy task and is one that takes continual adjustment to the stress and challenges in life. Balance is a dynamic process means you need to continually adjust your levels of closeness and flexibility.

Using a skiing analogy, a balanced couple relationship is not unlike skiing at a professional level. An accomplished skier keeps her legs about shoulder width apart, not too close and not too far apart. Her knees are slightly bent, and each leg can flex independently of the other, based on the conditions. She does not lean too far forward or too far backward on her skis, allowing for optimal balance. Her arms extend slightly in front of her body, comfortably holding her ski poles, which are lightly planted in the snow as she initiates each turn with refined rhythm and timing. This form allows the skier to maintain stability and control despite changing conditions. Her legs will flex in moguls, allowing her upper body to stay calm and balanced. The expert skier can also make subtle but important changes in her position to maintain her balance and ability to carve a smooth turn even as a slope becomes steeper, the snow becomes deeper, or the conditions become icy. Balanced couples operate in a similar manner. They are two independent individuals working together in a balanced way to stay connected and effectively adjust to whatever life throws their way.

A beginning skier is more like an unbalanced couple. There is tension in his body as he rigidly tries to hold form without falling. Stiff knees and an overly wide stance typically characterize his posture. Often, he leans too far forward or backward on his skies, throwing off his balance. His poles hang at his sides with no real function as he awkwardly tries to maintain control and check his speed. Even if he finds comfort on the beginner hills, any change in the conditions is sure to cause problems. He is not able to adjust to ice, moguls, deep powder, or steeper hills. This lack of form dramatically limits his options for exploring and enjoying an entire ski area.

Unbalanced couples are similar to these beginning skiers. They are rigid and struggle to make adjustments when under stress or when things don't go as planned. They can get stuck in one place and use the same strategy over and over again, even when it doesn't work for them. Stress and challenges can cause them to falter, driving them apart rather than bringing them together as a team.

They say that the earlier you start skiing, the easier it is to learn. Young skiers don't have bad habits to overcome and are seldom afraid of falling and getting hurt. A good teacher giving ski lessons can also make a big difference. The same is true for learning to balance closeness and flexibility in your relationship. If your parents modeled a good balance of closeness and flexibility from very early on, you likely grew up in a stable and loving family environment. Finding a balanced relationship in your marriage will be easier because it will come naturally for you. If, on the other hand, you did not have healthy role models, you may have bad habits to overcome. Some will have painful memories of dysfunctional relationships. You'll need to learn balanced closeness and flexibility as an adult. It may take more work and practice.

ILLUSTRATIONS OF UNBALANCED FAMILIES FROM THE MOVIES AND TELEVISION

Movies and television shows often portray unbalanced couples and families because they are more dramatic, interesting, and sometimes comical. The following popular examples illustrate several unbalanced types.

The television series *Everybody Loves Raymond* represents an unbalanced family that is "overly connected" and "inflexibile" (lower right corner of the map). Ray is a successful sportswriter living on Long Island with his wife, Debra, and their three children. Ray's parents live directly across the street, and it enables them to continually intrude on them as a couple—hence the overly connected family. Ray's brother, Robert, is a divorced policeman, and he often visits also. Ray's mother, Marie, is the matriarch of the family and is in everyone's business, continually trying to control everyone else. Debra hopelessly tries to find some space and autonomy from Ray's parents but is usually unsuccessful. The entire family system is rigid and has difficulty trying to change or make improvements.

In the movie *What About Bob?* we observe an unbalanced family that is "disconnected" and "inflexible" (lower left corner of map). Dr. Leo Marvin is a prominent psychiatrist who is the author of a popular book called *Baby Steps*. His wife is Fay, and they have a teenage daughter, Anna, and nine-year-old son, Sigmund. The family members are emotionally disconnected from the father, and the couple also has a disconnected relationship. Leo is an authoritarian parent with rigid rules and little flexibility. Bob Wiley, played by Bill Murray, a client of Dr. Marvin, tracks Marvin's family down while they are on vacation and tries to join them. Bob brings closeness and flexibility to the family, which Dr. Marvin resents but the family loves. While Bob is with the family, they become closer and more flexible, making them more balanced despite Dr. Marvin's resistance. This demonstrates how the leadership in a family can dramatically impact the way a family operates. A shift in leadership can change the relationship patterns of all individuals in the family.

In the MTV series *The Osbournes*, we see an unbalanced family that is "overly flexible" (chaotic) and "overly connected" (top right corner of the map). Ozzy Osbourne is the former lead singer of the rock band Black Sabbath, and he lives with his wife, Sharon, two children, Jack and Kelly (daughter Aimee did not appear regularly on the show), and several dogs that are not house-trained. The teenagers are often rebellious and abuse drugs as they bring a whole range of friends through the house. Ozzy often appears to be on drugs himself, and Sharon appears to be more connected to the dogs than the family. There are only feeble, inconsistent attempts at discipline, and the children and all family members fluctuate between being emotionally disconnected and emotionally enmeshed. They are very dysfunctional and are an excellent example of an unbalanced family.

CHANGES IN COUPLES AND FAMILIES OVER TIME

Couple and family relationships change over time, and the Couple and Family Map is a useful way to illustrate these changes. Like the river flowing, relationships change in their levels of closeness and flexibility to better adapt to the issues that occur over time. The story of the following family demonstrates how much change can occur in relationships and that where you are today is not where you will be in a few years.

Jerry and Diane began dating in college (1), and their relationship was "very connected" and "very flexible" as they were enjoying getting to know each other. As newlyweds (2) their relationship was "overly connected" as they were very much in love and were "somewhat flexible" as they led a rather structured life where they were both very busy developing their own careers. After five years of marriage (3), they were perfectly balanced on both closeness and flexibility. They became somewhat less emotionally connected and more flexible as a couple because of the demands of work.

The birth of their first baby (4) created a dramatic change in their relationship, especially since their child, Anna, had colic and Jerry was traveling more often with his new job. Diane was often exhausted, and they felt things were often out of control ("overly flexible"); however, meeting the demands of a newborn kept them "very connected." When Anna was in preschool (5), the family was more structured ("somewhat flexible") as Jerry was more available and they were feeling generally connected in their marriage. They struggled with the challenges of Anna's adolescent years (6) as she was rebelling at home and at school, and they felt things were out of control ("very flexible") and the family was not feeling very close to each other ("somewhat close").

The changes in closeness and flexibility that both the marriage and the family experienced over time is normal, and it is in many ways useful as people deal with the demands of life. This clearly illustrates that even in healthy relationships the dynamics are going to change, and that should be expected. A good exercise for you and your partner to do is to plot how your relationship

FIGURE 9.6

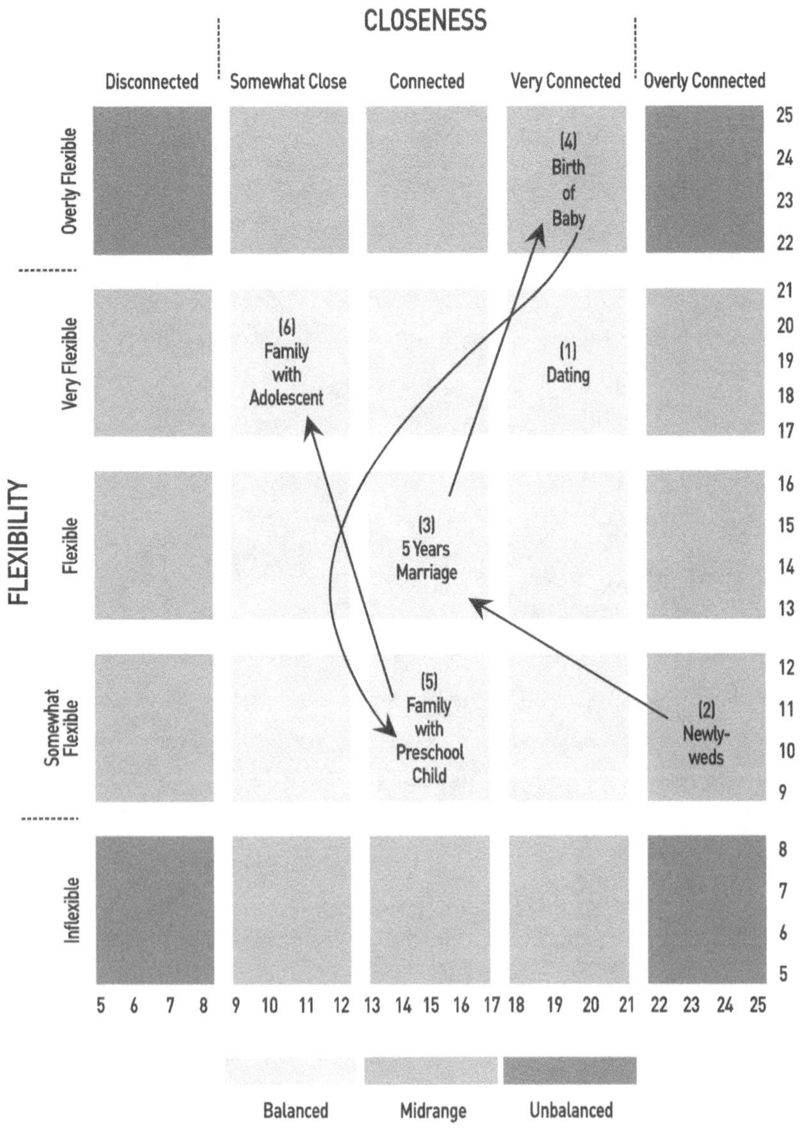

CLOSENESS

has changed over time. It is interesting to note how the pattern of changes on the map is unique to each couple, so it will be up to you to explore how your relationship has developed.

> If you have taken the **Online Couple Checkup,** the results for you and your partner are graphed onto the Couple Map. Along with your results are questions and suggestions for discussing how you each see your relationship in terms of closeness and flexibility.
>
> If you do not plan to take the Couple Checkup, you can complete the exercise below.

COUPLE EXERCISE 9.1
Couple Map Quiz

You can take this Couple Map Quiz alone and see how you perceive your relationship. Encourage your partner to also take the quiz so you can identify your strengths and issues regarding closeness and flexibility as a couple.

Couple Closeness

- How often do you spend free time together?
    1. Never
    2. Seldom
    3. Sometimes
    4. Often
    5. Very Often

- How committed are you to your partner?
    1. Slightly
    2. Somewhat
    3. Generally
    4. Very
    5. Extremely

- How close do you feel to your partner?

    1. Not very close

    2. Somewhat close

    3. Generally close

    4. Very close

    5. Extremely close

- How do you and your partner balance separateness and togetherness?

    1. Mainly separateness

    2. More separateness than togetherness

    3. Equally

    4. More togetherness than separateness

    5. Mainly togetherness

- How independent of or dependent on each other are you and your partner?

    1. Very independent

    2. More independent than dependent

    3. Equally dependent and independent

    4. More dependent than independent

    5. Very dependent

Add the numbers that correspond with each of your responses to get your total closeness score.

Couple Flexibility

- What kind of leadership is there in your couple relationship?

    1. One person usually leads

    2. Leadership is sometimes shared

    3. Leadership is generally shared

    4. Leadership is usually shared

    5. Leadership is unclear

- How often do you and your partner do the same things (roles) around the house?
    1. Almost always
    2. Usually
    3. Often
    4. Sometimes
    5. Seldom

- What are the rules (written or unwritten) like in your relationship?
    1. Rules are very clear and very stable
    2. Rules are clear and generally stable
    3. Rules are clear and structured
    4. Rules are clear and flexible
    5. Rules are unclear and changing

- How are decisions made?
    1. One person usually decides
    2. Decisions are sometimes shared
    3. Decisions are often shared
    4. Decisions are usually shared
    5. Decisions are rarely made

- How much change occurs in your couple relationship?
    1. Very little change
    2. Little change
    3. Some change
    4. Considerable change
    5. A great deal of change

Add the numbers that correspond with each of your responses to these questions to get your total flexibility score.

COUPLE EXERCISE 9.2
Exercise on Couple Map

1. Complete the Couple Map Quiz for how your relationship is *now*. Then take the quiz again to describe how you would *ideally* like your couple relationship to be.

2. Score the quiz for both the "now" and the "ideal." Then plot both scores onto the Couple and Family Map (see Figure 9.5).

		Closeness	Flexibility
Partner 1			
	Now		
	Ideal		
Partner 2			
	Now		
	Ideal		

3. Compare how you each described your relationship *now* on the Couple and Family Map. Discuss similarities and differences on couple closeness and couple flexibility.

4. Compare how you each described how you would *ideally* like your relationship to be. Discuss similarities and differences.

5. Discuss how you can work together to make your relationship more ideal for both partners.

SUGGESTIONS FOR IMPROVING YOUR COUPLE DYNAMICS

1. If you are not happy with the closeness in your relationship, talk about how you can achieve a more satisfying balance of separateness and togetherness.

2. If you are not happy with the flexibility of your relationship, discuss how you can achieve a more satisfying balance of stability and change.

3. Be aware that you will often repeat styles you learned from your family of origin, especially under stress. You can also discuss how you each perceive your relationship when you are each feeling stress.

Specific Suggestions for *Increasing* Couple Closeness

Spend more quality time together. Ideally these would be moments when you are communicating in an honest and open way, doing something you both enjoy. However, some couples also enjoy being together while doing separate activities, such as reading in the same room. Too often the couple relationship gets leftover time when one or both of you are exhausted.

Plan and dream together. Create a list of things you would like to do in your life and share your list with your partner. My (Amy's) husband and I have done this over the years (sometimes including our children) and have a lot of fun with it. It makes me feel closer to my husband when I understand his hopes and dreams, and it also creates a bond when we have found lists from the past and have seen some of our dreams come to fruition. Before we were married my husband gave me a beautiful empty photo album and wrote some of his dreams on blank pages, waiting for us to have photos of these anticipated events. Seeing this album with pages where he had written "marry Amy," "buy a house," and "have a baby" endears him to me and makes me look forward to dreaming and creating more memories together.

Fill in the blanks. Sometimes the simplest discussions have mysterious ways of deepening the connection you have with your partner. When my (Amy's) older daughter was in first grade, she brought home an assignment that was just a piece of paper filled with five large, empty circles. The topic was Fears, and she was to write five of her fears in these circles. She had already completed the assignment but would be given extras if her parents did it as well. One of my best friends was over at the time, so we made copies and all filled out our fears.

This particular evening is seared in my memory as a special time, and I have saved each of our "fear" sheets. When I take them out, it brings back the warm memories of that evening and how such a simple activity enlivened our conversation, emphasizing our shared humanity through fears. I recently found and read these pages again and felt my heart smile. I remembered how my daughter wrote "running out of air" as one of her fears and my friend wrote "statistics," as she was completing her doctoral degree at the time. My husband had written "war" and "someone I love dying," which capture his caring nature.

When we know someone's fears, our hearts open even more to them, but fear is just one of many possible topics for discussion. A page of blank circles can be filled in with any number of simple statements or questions, such as, "I appreciate . . ." or "A favorite memory of mine is . . ." The point is to have a specialized discussion from the heart rather than talking about people, events, or things.

Other Suggestions for Increasing Couple Closeness

- Say no to outside activities that take too much time and energy away from your relationship.
- Participate in community service or volunteer projects together.
- Start having a weekly date night.
- Take a class or vacation together.
- Find a hobby or activity you can share with one another.

Specific Suggestions for Balancing Separateness and Togetherness

Maintain, create, and nurture other social connections. The balance between personal space and couple closeness varies by individual. Very often partners have different desires for closeness as well as different modes to achieve this balance. For instance, women more frequently express the need for closeness through communication, while men describe shared recreational activities as a way to increase closeness. First of all, discuss with your partner how you each feel about your level of closeness. Extreme levels of closeness are normal for certain relational stages, and it may be that you are both very happy with this pattern. Keep in mind, however, that you may be overburdening your partnership while neglecting other important social connections such as family, friends, and community.

Men and women who have close relationships outside their marriage are mentally and physically healthier than those who rely on just their partner for emotional intimacy and support. Diversifying close relationships may actually strengthen your couple relationship by releasing the pressure on that relationship to fulfill many emotional needs. I (Amy) have to specifically carve out time to be with friends, even though my inclination is just to be at home. I am a homebody by nature. I can always find ways to occupy my time at home, and I just love to be there, especially with my husband, Daniel, and our children. Daniel is fun and easy to be with, and we have many activities, we both enjoy doing. I have noticed about myself that, when he is home, I rarely ever think to call a friend, and if a friend calls I feel the pull of being away from my family.

I can see how this can become a problem, and for me it appeared in the context of tennis. Tennis is one of my favorite activities and one that requires at least one other person to play. The weather in Minnesota limits the number of days I can play outdoor tennis, which somehow compels me to want to take advantage of them. Daniel loves to play tennis as well, but on one of those days when I was itching to play he hadn't wanted to join me. It was really hard for me to give up the idea of playing. I badgered him and tried to convince him to play with me. I even became irritated with him—feeling as though he was preventing me from doing something I really wanted to do!

I see tennis as analogous to interpersonal exchanges. In tennis, as in communication, you volley back and forth in a give-and-take. It is a dynamic process. Because I was dependent on Daniel to play tennis, I put unnecessary pressure on him and our relationship. For me the solution was in participating in tennis drills at the club where we belonged. This enabled me to play more tennis and also meet other people who enjoy playing. I also meet up with my parents, who like to play, and I have discovered a cousin who plays as well.

From a relational standpoint, and thinking about this in terms of decreasing couple closeness, my spending time playing tennis with other people benefits our couple relationship while improving my social life in the process. "Decreasing closeness" is almost a misnomer, because the emotional closeness is unaffected or even improved. The goal of increasing, maintaining, or nurturing other relationships is really to have a more level balance between "couple" time and time spent with others.

So again, talk with your partner about how satisfied you each are about your current level of closeness. Even if you are both satisfied with extreme closeness, be sure to not neglect other relationships—your personal, couple, and social life will ultimately benefit from a good balance.

Other Suggestions for Increasing Independence

- Take a class alone or with friends.

- Volunteer for something your partner is not involved with.

- Give yourself some alone time walking, jogging, or journaling. Get to know and like yourself. When your tank is full, you'll have more to share with your partner later.

Specific Suggestions for *Increasing* Couple Flexibility

Share leadership and roles. If you and your partner have strictly defined roles and leadership patterns, try changing the normal routine. In my (Amy's) family, I need to take periodic breaks from cooking. Like my grandmothers, I love to cook and to bake. Because it is one of the ways I like to nurture my family, I can get caught up in cooking to the point where it consumes most of my free time. I have definitely had times in my life when I was unbalanced in "me" time and when most of my waking hours were devoted to giving to my family in one form or another—and a lot of that time was spent cooking!

This problem revealed itself when a fast-food restaurant opened near our home about the time our son was old enough to walk there on his own. Since we do not eat at fast-food restaurants, this was a novelty for our son, and for a short time he was walking there almost daily after school. As could be expected, when I would present dinner, he was not hungry on the days he had eaten a sandwich and chips an hour or two earlier. I could not believe that the time, effort, and thought I put into our dinners were being replaced by Jimmy John's!

After several months of this happening frequently, I realized my behavior was part of the problem. When every night had to have a dinner party–quality meal, family members who were not hungry felt like no-show dinner guests. I felt frustrated and unappreciated. I was spending too much time and placing too much importance on the content of the meals. Feeling personally insulted when my son wasn't hungry was a major indicator of the unhealthy pattern into which I had slipped. The cognitive aspect of resolving this issue for me was to realize the impracticality of my high expectations. Behaviorally, I needed to have other creative outlets than cooking.

The way I approached role sharing in cooking was made easier because it coincided nicely with the developmental stages of my children. The two oldest are now teenagers, perfectly capable of finding something to prepare on their own. We have talked a lot about having them take turns planning and cooking a family meal, as my brothers and I did as teens. I must admit that this is merely lip service at the moment, although we *have* enjoyed meals they prepared for their foods class homework. My husband is responsible for dinner at least one night a week, when I take yoga with a friend. We still have family meals together most evenings, but they are simpler. I will often go a whole weekend or even longer without cooking at all. None of us is malnourished, and I am happier and have more time when cooking is not completely my responsibility.

Other Suggestions for Increasing Flexibility

- Put away your lists, calendars, and schedules for a week. Learn what it is like to not be so structured all the time.

- Brainstorm a list of your roles, rules, and expectations for your marriage and family. Revise this list in a way that increases flexibility.

- Switch roles with your partner for a week. If your partner normally does the grocery shopping, you do it this week.

- Do something really spontaneous (i.e. clear your schedule for a day or week and use that time to meet your partner for a romantic getaway).

Specific Suggestions for Adding Stability and Structure

Add more consistency, tradition, and ritual. While flexibility is a very important characteristic of happy couples, it does not undermine the importance of ritual and routine. Flexibility is an adaptive response to the unpredictability of life, but when flexibility becomes *characteristic* of the relationship, the risk of instability is great. Think for a minute about your warmest memories from childhood or adolescence. Most likely you will remember not an isolated event but something that, through repetition and predictability, became a ritual. My (Amy's) warmest childhood memories are two common but powerful rituals: the bedtime ritual and the mealtime ritual. I particularly remember my grandmother holding my hands and teaching me bedtime prayers, and dinners were always a happy time to reconnect with my parents and brothers.

Your couple relationship can benefit from the structure of routines and rituals too. Research has found that rituals and routines are important to individual health and well-being and are associated with marital satisfaction, stronger family relationships, and academic achievement for children.[4] Rituals powerfully bond and build loving relationships and are organizers of family life. During times of stress and transition, couples can retreat into the stability of their routines rather than flail about, causing more stress.

In addition to the mealtime and bedtime rituals, there are several other simple but powerful rituals you can incorporate into your couple and family life: the welcome home ritual and the good-bye ritual. According to David Quigley, the critical element of the good-bye ritual is the promise of return.[5] When you are parting for the day, a kiss good-bye along with the specific intention of your anticipated time of reconnecting makes this ritual simple. "Have a good day. I have a meeting until five o'clock. I'll be home at five thirty."

The welcome home ritual is another important way to connect with your partner. My husband and I (Amy) began consistently implementing this ritual into our lives, and it has provided such a stable sense of joy for us. We normally take a walk with the dog and process our day and upcoming plans. In the past there was often this chaos once everyone was home—the dog was running about excitedly and the children were vying to be heard. We would often just greet each other across the room amidst all this activity. Now we take our walk or a bike ride, and *then* we are able to focus on the family because we have had "our" time. It also centers us as parenting partners, because we have already had a chance to talk together about any issues the children may have.

Other Suggestions for Increasing Structure

- Make a list of household roles, rules, and expectations. Negotiate these with your partner.
- Write down a to-do list for the week and stick to it.
- Add more consistency to your parenting (if you have children).
- Keep promises made to your partner.

PARENTING— CREATING A BALANCED FAMILY

Before I got married, I had six theories about bringing up children; now I have six children, and no theories.

—JOHN WILMOT

THE ULTIMATE RESPONSIBILITY

Counselor Jennifer James's remark that "the first half of our lives is spoiled by our parents, and the last half by our children" humorously typifies the mixed blessing felt by many parents. People often refer to parenting as the most frustrating and the most rewarding experience in their lives. This is no wonder: parenting is a responsibility like no other. Parents are primarily responsible for their children's development of self-esteem, sense of responsibility, values, and physical and emotional health, as well as their social and economic needs. In spite of the monumental responsibilities associated with parenthood, people receive little, if any, training in parenting.

The good news: you are proactively engaged in the single most important thing you can do for your children: modeling the importance of your relationship. Studies have shown that a harmonious marriage relationship promotes competence and maturity in children.[1] Every bit of energy you put into supporting each other lovingly and respectfully will come back to you through your children. Whether you realize it or not, children are always observing and taking in your relationship. Their interpretation of how their parents interact with one another serves as a model for how they interact with others. Of course, they will learn experientially through their own relationships, but the parental dyad is a powerful template for the behaviors that will feel natural to them.

COMMON PROBLEMS RELATED TO PARENTING

"Don't worry that children never listen to you; worry that they are always watching you."

ROBERT FULGHAM

I (Peter) remember a time when my son, Adam, who was just a one-year-old at the time, taught me about the power of parent-child modeling. It was the holiday season, and we began to find coasters from the family room coffee table, under the Christmas tree. At first we assumed these had fallen off the coffee table by accident, so we put them back. But each day my wife and I would continue to find coasters scattered under the tree. It was very confusing. Finally, we noticed Adam playing with the coasters and putting them under the tree. It was at that moment the truth of the situation became clear to me.

The week before, when I was setting up the tree, Adam had watched intently as I worked on placing it in the stand. At first the tree was crooked, and I grabbed a coaster off the table and tried propping up one side of the stand to straighten things out. I was not satisfied with that fix, so I quickly put it away and adjusted the trunk of the tree by hand.

That one model of placing a coaster under the tree was all Adam needed to begin imitating this action. He did not even understand why his father had done it, but that didn't seem to matter. He chose to do what had been modeled for him.

Children are great imitators of all kinds of behaviors, not just positive ones. This is the flip side of being a relationship model for your children: they do not discriminate between desired and undesired behaviors. Children who grow up witnessing verbal or physical abuse between their parents often choose relationships where this dysfunction is repeated. More obscure, but still harmful, are the array of behaviors they may observe between parents that limit a relationship from reaching true intimacy. Some of these behaviors may be invalidating one another's feelings, withdrawing or avoiding, denying responsibility, and inattention. Children are always observing and internalizing their parents' example of how to act relationally. Dysfunctional patterns of interaction are a childhood wound passed on through the generations. The past is transmitted through the present to the future.

This need not be a continuing chronicle, however. Modeling a healthy and happy marriage is a gift to yourself and to your children. Learning about your relationship, improving it, and nurturing it can be thought of as benefiting not only your individual happiness but that of your children, their future children, and the larger community. It sets up a healthy cycle of relationship patterns—for today and extending into the future.

What intimacy obstacles do married people often encounter that are related to parenting? The major parenting issues in our national sample of fifty thousand married couples with children are identified in Figure 10.1. The most problematic parenting issue that couples report is feeling less satisfied in their marriage since having children. Over two-thirds of married couples report that the father does not spend enough time with the children. Almost as many couples do not agree on how to discipline their children and are dissatisfied with how child-care responsibilities are shared. Finally, many couples are dissatisfied with the balance of attention given to their marriage versus the attention given to the children. Let's look at each of these in a little more detail before taking steps to improve this area of your relationship.

FIGURE 10.1

Top Five Parenting Issues for Couples

Parenting Issue	Percentage of Couples Having Problem*
1. Having children has reduced our marital satisfaction.	82%

2. The father is not involved enough with our children.	**65%**
3. My partner focuses more on the children than on the marriage.	**64%**
4. I am dissatisfied with how child rearing is shared.	**64%**
5. We disagree on discipline.	**63%**

* One or both partners indicated this was an issue for them.

Strain on the Couple Relationship

Having children intensifies the couple bond, enriching and deepening the couple connection. But the enormous change and demands a child brings to the lives of his parents puts strain on the couple relationship. The time and energy necessary to parent often draws away from the couple's time and energy. Much of the nurturing that used to be directed toward one another now is directed at the child. Having children also means having a whole new set of responsibilities and roles, which need to be negotiated. For all of these reasons, parenting is one of the most challenging and stressful areas of a couple's relationship. Over four-fifths of the married couples in our national survey report feeling less satisfied in their marriage since having children. Even happily married couples are not immune from the stresses and strains associated with child rearing. Less than two-fifths of happily married couples report that children do not create major problems in their marriage.

The Husband's Lack of Involvement

The sacrifices related to parenting are felt most often by mothers. Women adapt their careers, sacrifice their free time, and otherwise adjust their lives to accommodate children considerably more than husbands do. A survey of fifteen hundred adults living in England examined the quality-of-life sacrifices parents make and how it affects their perception of parenting. Forty-one percent of fathers and 66 percent of mothers reported that their children are a major source of life happiness for them.[2] The woman's high value in parenting is especially interesting in light of the fact that she is penalized more in the form of sleep deprivation, social events missed, being passed over for promotions, and so on. This confirms that analytical calculations can never truly account for the experience between parent and child.

A major review of studies on the transition couples experience once they are parents found that both individuals had a decrease in marital satisfaction, increase in stress levels, and more differences than before.[3] But the decrease in marital satisfaction was twice as large for women as for men and was attributed to the woman's feelings that the partner is less involved than they are in dealing with child care and housework. Likewise, in our national survey, for a majority (65 percent) of couples, one or both partners indicated that the father does not spend enough time with the children.

Part of the problem may be that men feel their responsibilities primarily lie outside of the home. They may not have had a good role model in their own youth with a father actively involved in his children's daily lives. Some men falsely assume that child rearing is simply women's work.

Disagreements over Discipline and Parenting Styles

Nurturing the young to adulthood requires parents to be cognizant of the values they want to promote in their children, the behaviors they expect, and how to achieve these objectives. Becoming parents dramatically complicates the marital relationship as a shift occurs from fun and good feelings to responsibilities and decision making. Even if partners have the same vision for their child, how they choose to parent and discipline can be very different. This is because, unless there is a conscious effort to do differently, we tend to repeat with our own children the ways in which we were parented. Sixty-three percent of married couples in our survey disagree on how they handle discipline with their children. Not only can this be an irritant in the marital dyad, but it can be a problem with the child. Discipline that is not consistent, either with one parent or between parents, is not effective.[4]

Children Taking Priority over the Marriage

Children naturally will draw energy and resources away from couple time, but when children become the main focus of family life, the marriage can suffer. A majority (64 percent) of married couples report that partners give more attention to the children than to the marriage. One reason this is so common is that children are demanding—their needs are evident. Although spouses also have needs, they just are not as apparent as the needs of their children. Also, parents may feel as if they are acting selfishly if they ask for things for themselves. Ultimately, by the time one or both parents are finished taking care of the children, they have little time or energy left for each other or for the marriage.

FIGURE 10.2
Parenting Styles Family Map

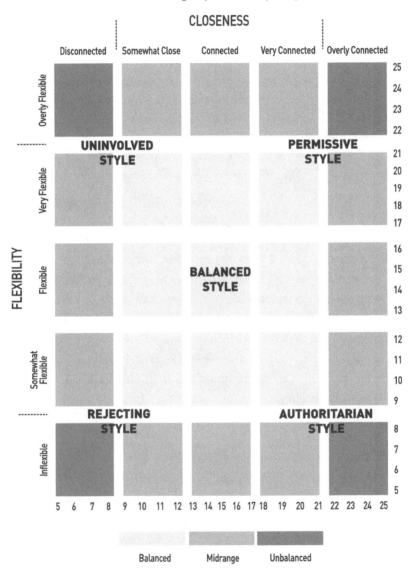

FIVE STYLES OF PARENTING

Differing ideas about how best to parent is an issue for many couples. Diana Baumrind has done considerable research on parenting styles and has identified four styles of parenting: democratic (which we call "balanced"), authoritarian, permissive, and rejecting.[5] We added the uninvolved style, which was adapted from the Parenting Styles Family Map (see Figure 10.2).

Discuss the following questions with your partner:

1. How were you parented as a child and teen? Did your mother and father use the same or different parenting styles? What are your reactions to their style? Did it feel fair? Was it effective?

2. What style feels most natural to you as a parent? Is this the same style you would like to use?

3. What concerns do you have about your partner's parenting behavior?

As we discuss each parenting style, we will describe the typical behavior that has been found in children raised by each style. Figure 10.3 summarizes the five parenting styles and children's consequent behaviors. Remember, these are generalized patterns that have been found over several hundred studies and there will always be exceptions to these patterns.

FIGURE 10.3
Parenting Styles and Children's Behaviors

Parenting Style	Children's Behavior
Balanced	Energetic and friendly
	Self-reliant and cheerful
	Achievement-oriented
Authoritarian	Unfriendly
	Conflicted and irritable
	Unhappy and unstable

Parenting Style	Children's Behavior
Permissive	Impulsive and rebellious
	Low-achieving
Rejecting	Immature
	Psychologically troubled
Uninvolved	Lonely and withdrawn
	Low-achieving

Balanced Parenting

In balanced parenting, parents establish clear rules and expectations and discuss them with the child. Although they acknowledge the child's perspective, they are the authority, using both reason and power to enforce their standards. Being an authority is different than being controlling. When a controlling person tries to enforce her values, she makes a lot of noise, fighting for power. When you are truly an authority, there is no fight. No noise is necessary. In fact, you can set the tone with your calmness. Often when balanced parents are challenged, saying nothing can have all the influence in the world. In terms of closeness, parents who use a balanced approach have a warm, loving relationship with their children without smothering them.

The balanced style is represented by the center position on Figure 10.2. Balanced families, therefore, tend to range from "somewhat connected" to "very connected" on the closeness dimension and from "somewhat flexible" to "very flexible" on the flexibility dimension. Considerable research on parenting has demonstrated that more balanced families have children who are more emotionally healthy and happy and are more successful in schol and life. Children of balanced-style parents exhibit what Baumrind describes as energetic-friendly behavior. These children are very self-reliant and cheerful, they cope well with stress, and they are achievement oriented.

Authoritarian Parenting

In authoritarian parenting, parents have rigid rules and expectations and strictly enforce them. These parents expect and demand obedience from their children. The authoritarian style is located in the lower right quadrant of Figure 10.2, indicating a somewhat-flexible to inflexible family system and a very connected or overly connected family system. As the authoritarian style becomes more intense, the family moves toward the unbalanced style called "inflexible and overly connected." This type of family system is particularly problematic for adolescents, who tend to rebel against this style of parenting. In Baumrind's studies, children of authoritarian-style parents are often conflicted and irritable in behavior; they tend to be moody, unhappy, vulnerable to stress, and unfriendly.

Permissive Parenting

In permissive parenting, parents let the child's preferences take priority over their own ideals and rarely force the child to conform to their standards. The permissive style is located in the upper right quadrant of Figure 10.2, indicating families that are very flexible to overly flexible and very connected to overly connected. As the permissive style becomes more extreme, the family moves toward the "overly flexible, overly connected," also called "chaotically enmeshed," style. The chaotically enmeshed style is problematic in parenting because the constant change and forced togetherness is not healthy for children. Baumrind observed that children of permissive-style parents generally exhibit impulsive-aggressive behavior. These children tend to be rebellious, domineering, and low achievers.

Rejecting Parenting

In rejecting parenting, parents do not pay much attention to their child's needs and seldom have expectations regarding how the child should behave. The rejecting style is located in the lower left quadrant of Figure 10.2, indicating families that tend to range from somewhat-flexible to inflexible and from somewhat-connected to disconnected. As the rejecting style becomes more extreme, the family moves toward the "inflexibly disconnected" style. This style makes it difficult for children to feel cared for, yet they are expected to behave because there are many rules. As a result, children from these homes are often immature and have psychological problems.

Uninvolved Parenting

In uninvolved parenting, parents often ignore the child, letting the child's preferences prevail as long as those preferences do not interfere with the parents' activities. The uninvolved style of parenting is located in the upper left quadrant of Figure 10.2, indicating a family that is somewhat-connected to disconnected and is very flexible to overly flexible. As the uninvolved style becomes more extreme, it moves toward the "overly flexible, disconnected" pattern. This pattern is problematic for children because they are left on their own without emotional support or consistent rules and expectations. The uninvolved style of parenting is not often discussed in published research, but in many instances it is combined with the rejecting style. Children of uninvolved parents are often withdrawn loners and low achievers.

PARENTING STRENGTHS OF HAPPY COUPLES

Our national survey of fifty thousand couples identified some parenting-related differences between happily and unhappily married couples. Figure 10.4 summarizes the findings. Let's examine some of these and look at lessons learned from happily married couples.

Making the Couple Relationship a Priority

Although children take a lot of energy and attention, it is essential for the survival of the marriage that spouses not forget about each other and their relationship. Parenthood has an amazing way of bringing out the selflessness in people; children's needs and desires often come before those of the parents. And although you may not mind this at all, it is important for your children and for your relationship to make your marriage a priority.

Indeed, a strength of happy couples is that they are about twice as likely (59 percent) as unhappy couples (31 percent) to report that their partners give as much attention to the marriage as they do the children. Taking time each day to share the day's events and to connect with each other is important. You need to take initiative in planning your time together. If your marriage is going to be satisfying, it cannot be left to chance. And your children will benefit from the effort you put into your marital relationship. You and your spouse are critical role models as your children's prototype for how partners relate to one another and what it means to be married. A happy marriage is a priceless gift to your children.

FIGURE 10.4
Strengths of Happy Couples versus Unhappy Couples Regarding Parenting

Parenting Issue	Percentage in Agreement	
	Happy Couples	Unhappy Couples
1. I am satisfied with how child rearing is shared.	61%	30%
2. My partner focuses as much on our marriage as on the children.	59%	31%
3. We agree on discipline.	59%	33%
4. We feel closer since having children.	53%	33%
5. I am more satisfied in my marriage since having children.	35%	19%

Recognizing That Parenting Is a Team Effort

As Figure 10.4 shows, satisfaction with how the responsibility of raising children is shared is the most significant issue distinguishing happy couples from unhappy ones. Happily married couples are twice as likely (61 percent) to be satisfied with how child rearing and parenting are shared than unhappily married couples (30 percent).

Co-parenting is simply a team approach to parenting. Co-parenting involves sharing all aspects of the child's growth and is based on the principle that the commitment and devotion of each parent is necessary to raise a well-adjusted child. Each parent has something unique to offer his or her children. Best of all, researchers have found that co-parenting improves both the marital relationship and the relationship between parent and child. Parenthood is much too important and much too time-consuming to be left to one person.

> "It's time for us to turn to each other, not on each other."
>
> JESSE JACKSON

Another important benefit of co-parenting is that it brings fathers into the family on an emotional level. Some observers have concluded that fathers often "draw on their life at home to take care of their emotional needs, but . . . distance themselves from the emotional needs of other family members."[6] Some fathers enjoy being nurtured at home but are not willing to nurture others in the home or feel they do not have the capacity to do so. The experience of co-parenting can help men learn how to attend to the emotional needs of others. This is a skill that has often been neglected because our culture tends to socialize men for competition, not cooperation.

Develop a Life Outside of Your Children

One possible problem with co-parenting is that sometimes the marriage gets lost in the shuffle. Often, the mother is working outside the home, caring for the children, doing housework; the father is doing the same. Two outside full-time jobs and the job of maintaining a family and household add up to at least three full-time jobs for only two people. Often the marriage is neglected while the spouses concentrate on their employment responsibilities and their family and household tasks. The couple might be doing great at the office and great with the kids, but they still end up getting divorced because they forgot to focus on their relationship with each other. They need to remember that the foundation for the whole operation is a strong marriage.

The following scenario is commonly seen by marriage and family therapists. John and Kristen have been married for thirteen years.

They report the first few years of their marriage as being very sat-isfying. By the time they seek therapy, they report a disconnection from one another, but they are overall very happy with their family and social lives. John and Kristen have two children, ages eight and ten. They report that they seldom spend time with just each other, as their spare time is spent either at their children's activi-ties or together as a family. Couple intimacy is almost nonexistent: when they have moments without the children, their conversations are almost always about the children or household management. John reports that Kristen is a wonderful mother, devoted to the children and to their emotional, physical, and spiritual growth. Kristen also compliments John's parenting, family devotion, and character.

In their admirable dedication to their children, they have lost touch with their own bond and relationship, and in fact, minimize its importance. While their children are thriving in the quality time they receive from their parents, they are witnesses to a mar-riage where the couple relationship is not nurtured as the heart of the family. More than likely, this is the kind of marriage John and Kristen's children will unconsciously re-create someday for themselves. John and Kristen may want to ask themselves: are we modeling the kind of marriage we want for our children?

One of the offerings of parenthood is the surprising ease in surrender-ing our own wills to the good of our children. Most parents freely choose to reduce or even abandon their interests outside of their family life. After all, it is wildly entertaining and satisfying to spend time with your children. In fact, when asked if John and Kristen spend time away from the children, Kristen replied, "We are enjoying our children so much; I have no desire to pawn them off to a baby-sitter or grandparent." The problem with this logic is twofold: maintaining the priority of your marriage is good for your marriage *and* for your children. Babies will be children, children will be teenagers, and teens will grow to be adults. Part of the growing-up process for teenagers will be a desire to separate from parents and experience their own individuality. Parenthood has sometimes been characterized as a long process of letting go. Children irrefutably benefit from reliable warmth, free-flowing communication, and parental involvement, but give your child the gift of knowing he or she is not your whole life.

John and Kristen found it initially difficult leaving their children to spend time alone with each other, and the children wanted to know why they were not invited too. The first few times they had dates, they even had a difficult time talking about anything other than their home lives and their children. Their therapist reminded them that the point of these dates was not to recapture their lives before children but to expand and validate their relationship alongside their roles as mom and dad to their children. Over time their dates felt natural and nourishing, and they used this time to learn new things together. The children resisted baby-sitters, but eventually they discovered a natural competency for adapting and connecting with alternative caregivers, be it a neighborhood baby-sitter or Grandma and Grandpa.

Supporting Each Other

Researchers often find higher levels of marital satisfaction in child-free marriages than in marriages with children. However, this difference is not significant with parents who get along well and have a strong commitment to co-parenting.

Parenting is demanding, and one way to help each other and to show you care is through mutual support. One way to be supportive is through parenting together. Another way is to continue building on your marriage and your lives. For example, continue dating your partner. As a couple, you need to fight for time to be together.

It is important to maintain your friendship with your partner as well. In addition, you should share some of your everyday experiences with your children. Parents commonly ask their children about their day while neglecting to share their own stories. If you talk to your children about your friends, job, activities, dreams, and concerns, they will be more likely to share their lives with you. By making a conscious effort to maintain and create a happy marriage and personal lives, you will be better parents.

Showing Love Through Discipline

Happily married couples are much more likely to agree on discipline than are unhappily married couples. Thus, it's important to discuss and develop a joint plan for discipline. It sounds so basic, but the fact is many couples disagree on how to discipline their children.

Children quickly pick up on differences in parenting, and they may manipulate parents or direct their requests according to how they have learned each parent will respond. A simplistic but classic example illustrates this phenomenon. Suppose young Dylan asks his mother if he can have a cookie. His mother might respond, "I would like for you to wait until after dinner, since we will be eating soon and I want you to have room in your tummy for healthy food." Because Dylan is only four years old, he is not happy with his mother's reply—he wants that cookie *now*. So he seeks out his father and asks him if he can have a cookie. Dylan's father did not hear the exchange between Mom and Dylan, and he tells Dylan that he may have a cookie.

What Dylan has learned is that if one parent says no, he merely needs to ask the other parent. The cookie itself is harmless, but the lesson Dylan learns can have more serious implications later in life and ultimately make it more difficult to parent him. Therefore, you should frequently discuss discipline and parenting styles with your partner so that you can present a united front to your children.

You will also need to adjust your parenting style and disciplinary procedures according to the age of your children. When children are young they need parents to manage their lives, but as they grow parents must gradually relinquish their managerial skills and hone their consulting skills. At every stage of parenting it is important to have a consistent plan so that your children cannot play you and your spouse against each other. If children sense dissension, they may use it to divide you, hurting themselves in the process.

When it comes to discipline, do not worry about always being "right" or in having similar consequences as other parents. Discuss discipline with your partner and do as you agree feels right, and adjust and change as your children grow and develop. Not all of your decisions will be perfect, but it is important that when you make a decision, you stick with it. Children in the end will not remember the specifics of the situation, but they will remember that you cared enough to take a stand. It is their job to test boundaries and your job to reassure them that the boundaries are there.

Overindulgence

The issue of overindulging children is a timely and pertinent one. Many parents unintentionally harm their children by giving them too much—gifts, time, resources, and freedom. Jean Illsley Clarke, Connie Dawson, and David Bredehoft's book *How Much Is Enough?* provides thorough and excellent research on the issue of overindulgence. According to the authors, there are three different ways in which children are overindulged: by giving *too much*, by *over-nurturing*, and by *soft structure.*[7]

> "If you want children to keep their feet on the ground, put some responsibility on their shoulders."
>
> ABIGAIL VAN BUREN ("DEAR ABBY")

Giving *too much* not only refers to material items but also includes such things as too much entertainment, vacation, television, privileges, or lessons. In their research, adults who were overindulged by being given too much as children have a difficult time determining when they have had "enough" of something, whether it is food, clothing, work, sex, or television. These children and then adults do not learn to delay gratification and often do not feel competent in everyday life skills or their interpersonal relationships.

Over-nurturing refers to providing too much care—in the form of attention or performing acts for the child that he or she are capable of doing themselves. Like all forms of indulgence, over-nurturing is done with love and good intentions, but the outcome is that children do not learn age-appropriate developmental tasks. When parents do more than is necessary for their children, children tend to under-function. And when too much is done for children, they do not learn to be successful and confident in their own abilities.

The term *soft structure* was created by Clarke, Dawson, and Bredehoft to describe the third way in which parents overindulge children. Soft structure can include not having or not enforcing rules, shielding children from the consequences of their behavior, not insisting they do chores, or giving children too much freedom. In their research, adults who were overindulged with soft structure as children often reported that they were not expected to do chores when they were growing up. Chores are an important way for children to feel they are valued and contributing members of a household. They also provide an opportunity for children to learn life skills before they live on their own or with others.

They contend that overindulgence is a form of child neglect, because it "cripples your children's chances of becoming healthy, happy adults."[8] While overindulgence comes about with good intentions on the part of the parents, the consequences are detrimental to children. Children need the security of rules and limits. Their sense of self-worth comes from contributing to the greater good of the family and completing age-appropriate tasks on their own. They learn competency by doing for themselves; they learn patience, persistence, and deserving by learning to earn what they are given. If children do not have opportunities to deal with adversity and frustration as they are growing up in the safety of their families, how will they deal with life when it does not always go their way? Children need to learn how to deal with adversity and frustration as they are growing up or they will be without skills when they enter the real world of bosses, teachers, and friendships. These are the kinds of adults who have difficulty not being the center of attention or who have trouble taking personal responsibility for their decisions.

Overindulgence can occur in any family, regardless of how much money a family has. According to family scientist Bill Doherty in his book *Take Back Your Kids*, accommodating too much is common for American parents born in the second half of the twentieth century.[9] These individuals were raised in an era that de-emphasized social conformity. The contemporary buzz words for parents have been about promoting "self-esteem" and "individual initiative"; the implication being that in order to do so, parents need to lather children with praise, opportunities, and love. There is nothing wrong with praise, opportunities, or love, as long as they are balanced. Balance means that the child's social calendar does not interfere with family time or family rituals. Balance means that the child learns to give as well as to receive. And balance also means that children have time to just be children—unstructured time to think and play, and yes, even to be bored.

IT TAKES A VILLAGE

It is not only the responsibility of parents but all of humanity to reach out to the children and adolescents of the world. After all, children are quite literally our future. They are the future policymakers, doctors, professors, business owners, caretakers of the earth, and parents. Every neglectful or hateful act directed toward a child will someday be expressed in the form of anger, hate, or violence. Every loving act directed toward a child will return and be expressed as a loving act of hope, compassion, or kindness.

Any opportunity to interact with a child can be meaningful and significant, even if it may not appear to be so. Oprah Winfrey has spoken about a moment as a child when she was recognized by an adult woman; it was one of the most unforgettable moments in her life. The woman had just smiled and told her she was cute, but Oprah remembered feeling special and singled out. Years later she contacted this woman to thank her for this one simple comment. Think about how easy it can be to plant a seed of hope in the life of a child. Who doesn't have time to smile or find a positive way to recognize a child? If you have the freedom in your schedule, volunteer at a homeless shelter, a group home for youth, or a local school. There are so many ways to help build caring communities and futures. And the values we can impart in today's children and adolescents will be reflected in tomorrow's society.

> "Children are the living messages we send to a time we will not see."
>
> JOHN W. WHITEHEAD

Parenting as Peoplemaking

Virginia Satir coined the term "peoplemaking" as a euphemism for parenting.[10] As a parent, you play many roles, including nurse, storyteller, counselor, entertainer, encourager, organizer, nurturer, coach, and mediator. Each role is different in action but equal in importance. And as a parent, you are both teacher and student. What a glorious privilege it is to be such an important person in the life of a child. The following poem describes the importance of focusing on peoplemaking rather than more external things.

> One hundred years from now
> It will not matter
> What kind of car I drove,
> What kind of house I lived in,
> How much money I had in my bank account,
> Nor what my clothes looked like.
> But one hundred years from now
> The world may be a little better
> Because I was important
> In the life of a child.
>
> —ANONYMOUS

CHECK-IN PROCESS

Where are you *now*? (Identify and discuss your results.)

1. Review the Couple Checkup *individual* results. How satisfied were each of you in this area?

_____

_____

2. Review the Couple Checkup *couple* results. Was parenting a strength or growth area?

_____

_____

3. Discuss your agreement items (your strengths).

_____

_____

Where would you like to be? (Discuss issues.)

1. Review the discussion items in your Couple Checkup report.

2. Choose one issue you both want to resolve.

3. Share how you each feel about the issue.

How do you get there? (Develop your action plan.)

1. Brainstorm a list of ways to handle your parenting problems.

2. Agree on one solution you will try.

3. Decide what you will each do to make the plan work.

4. Review the progress in one week.

COUPLE EXERCISE 10.1
Planning a Weekly Family Conference

A family conference is a time for your family to connect and reflect on recent family and personal experiences. Spending this time together helps family members feel supported and gives a new energy and sense of solidarity to the family system.

1. Be sure that everyone participates.

2. Establish a regular time and place—perhaps following a time the entire family is normally together, such as after dinner.

3. Encourage and share ideas. Do not criticize or critique.

4. Have each family member discuss the following three questions:

   • What do you feel was the best thing that happened to you or happened within our family this week?

   • What was the worst thing that happened to you or within our family this week?

   • For an issue that was brought up in the last question, what could have been done differently?

REMINDERS FOR IMPROVING YOUR RELATIONSHIP AND PARENTING

1. Give attention to your marriage as well as to your children. Work hard to make sure you have time together without the children.

2. Discuss discipline styles and expectations with your partner.

3. Support each other in all aspects of parenting.

4. Be consistent and cooperative as a parenting team.

5. Never undermine your partner by critiquing or ridiculing their parenting in front of the children.

6. When rules have been established, both parents should consistently enforce them.

7. Do not allow your children to disrespect your partner.

ELEVEN

SCOPE OUT YOUR PERSONALITIES

*The goal of marriage is not to think alike,
but to think together.*

—R. DODD

No matter how much a couple has in common, it is impossible that two individuals would think, feel, and behave in exactly the same ways all the time. Not only are there gender and background differences, but every personality is unique. Exploring personality similarities and differences can be a fascinating and fun process. It can also shed light on the challenges faced by couples who love one another but have very different preferences in their approaches to life.

In addition, there are specific personality traits that can be more problematic within marriage than others. This chapter will begin by exploring general aspects of personality (found on the SCOPE Personality Scales page of your Couple Report) and include a discussion of specific personality attributes that predict with a high degree of accuracy high- and low-quality couple relationships.

PERSONALITY DEFINED

Before unpacking the personality traits identified by your Couple Checkup report, it is important to understand how personality is defined and understood. There are many ways to describe personality, and the academic definition differs greatly from what is usually thought of when we say a person has "personality." It is useful to think of personality as the characteristics of a person that lead to consistent patterns of feeling, thinking, and behaving.[1] This definition, while simple, generally provides a good framework from which to understand personality.

Another important aspect of personality is that it tends to be relatively stable over time. A common misperception is that you can change personality traits if you don't like them. While we might achieve slight adjustments in personality over time, our personality is pretty much set by the time we reach adolescence. For example, a goal-oriented person with high organizational abilities will exhibit these traits in many settings over her lifetime. She may never feel comfortable just letting things slide or doing something in a sloppy or careless way.

For couples, this means they should not try to change their partner, or expect their partner to change on their own. Relationship skills can be learned and improved. An individual can learn to communicate or manage finances more effectively. But an extrovert should not be expected to somehow become an introvert. An emotional person will likely always feel things more intensely than their less-emotional partner. Couples who set out to change one another's personalities will embark on a journey of frustration.

John and Sally had been married for three years. After a full week of work, John loved to come home and have some down time. He often felt the need to "zone out" for a while, with limited conversation and activity. Watching a movie or reading a book was a natural way for him to relax and recharge, and it was just what his introverted personality craved. Sally had recently transitioned from her professional career to staying home with their baby. By the time the weekend arrived, she often felt isolated and longed for adult conversation and contact. For her, recharging involved social interaction and visiting with friends and family. She often invited others over for dinner or arranged an outing for she and John to meet with friends. For Sally, talking and laughing with lots of friends around was what her extroverted personality longed for.

This difference was something that originally had attracted them to one another while they were dating. John appreciated Sally's energy and ability to talk to anybody. She had many friends and got him to be more active with others. Sally was impressed with how thoughtful and deep John was. He seemed very mature and down to earth. But as is often the case, personality differences that initially attract eventually attack. As John and Sally's marriage progressed, these personality differences often led to conflict, misunderstandings, and hurt feelings. Sally would make plans with friends, only to have John push back, refusing "another outing." Sally couldn't figure out why he was always saying no to her fun plans. John didn't understand why Sally couldn't appreciate a quiet afternoon just relaxing with a book. More and more, they started to drift apart as Sally would go out with her friends in the evenings and weekends, leaving John home alone with the baby.

IS THERE ROOM FOR BOTH PERSONALITIES ON OUR TEAM?

If we can't change one another's personality, what do we do with our differences? Before John and Sally took their Checkup, they did not really understand or appreciate their personality differences. Their tendency was that of most individuals: to try to make the other person think, feel, and behave the "right way"—more like them. It is very easy to slip into a critical mode when your partner displays very different lifestyle preferences and behavior.

- Why does she get so emotional about everything?
- Why can't he put his clothes in the hamper?
- I wish she would stand up for herself.
- How can he get so excited about every new idea that comes along?
- She never wants to do anything with our friends.

A good team is made up of individuals with strengths and abilities that are different from one another. A good baseball team needs not only a pitcher who throws well but other players who can hit and catch the ball. Great football teams have not only a solid quarterback leading the offense but other players who can run, catch, block, and tackle.

Marriage represents another type of team that requires a range of skills and responsibilities to be successful. Rather than focusing on the ways we wish we were more alike or the things we'd like to change in one another, couples can learn to understand, appreciate, and work with their personality differences. Let the more organized person tackle the task of balancing the checkbook. Allow the more assertive person to negotiate a major purchase. While the person who loves change and new ideas will keep you up to date, the more conventional person can help your team stay grounded and make balanced decisions.

There is no right or wrong combination of personality traits to form a successful relationship. While some couples may have an easier time blending their styles and preferences than others, in the end how you communicate, respect, and work with one another's differences will determine your relationship compatibility. Remember, your personality differences can be advantageous as you each bring unique abilities and perspectives to the relationship. Don't fall into the trap of criticizing one another's personality traits or trying to change someone to be something they are not. Instead, identify and discuss your similarities and differences and create solutions that allow you to work *with* one another rather than *against* one another.

But do more than just tolerate your personality differences. Celebrate them. In his book *Sustaining Love*, David Augsburger points out that on the way to mature love, most couples go through four stages.[2] First, during courtship, couples *accommodate* or tolerate one another's differences to avoid conflict and keep their dream relationship alive. After the wedding, when the reality of a spouse's personality sets in, partners try to *eliminate* the objectionable differences by criticizing or demanding change. However, when couples reach the third stage, they begin to *appreciate* the differences in personality as creative, necessary parts of the person they love *and* of the marriage itself. This paves the way for mature partners with a mature love to then *celebrate* and delight in their differences, recognizing that each is acceptable and beneficial to the health of the relationship.

BALANCE YOUR PERSONALITY STYLES

We've all seen people with extreme or out-of-balance personality styles: the girl who is so painfully shy she cannot make eye contact or hold a conversation; the guy who loves to party but can't seem to hold a job; the friend who is so committed to her goals that nothing else seems to matter; the relative who descends into anxiety or depression when things get stressful; or the person who stays up all night engaged in philosophical discussions on the future of politics—only to forget his important appointment the next morning. We should not use the fact that personality is made up of relatively permanent traits as an excuse for extreme or disruptive behavior in our lives.

The concept of *balance* applies not only to the flexibility and closeness in relationships but also to personality functioning. Once an individual understands their personality traits, they have the opportunity to begin making choices to ensure their behavior remains in balance. There is nothing wrong with being an introvert, but losing all contact with others or slipping into an aloof or alienated existence is out of balance. There is nothing wrong with being organized and goal directed, but neglecting your relationships with your spouse or children so you can focus on nothing but work or school is out of balance.

On a basic level, a personality trait is out of balance when it begins to interfere with work, school, your personal life, or relationships. Ask yourself, *Are there ways in which my personality is out of balance and interfering with other aspects of my life? What do I need to do to bring it back into balance?* You can even ask your partner what he or she thinks about the aspects of your personality that could be extreme. The Couple Checkup not only identifies your personality traits and styles but helps to define what an unbalanced personality trait looks like.

Not everyone has areas of their personality that push over into the extremes. But if you have a personality area that needs to be brought back into balance, begin to strategize and make behavioral choices that will help you avoid extreme expressions of that trait. Set realistic goals that will lead to more balanced behavior. For the couple described earlier in this chapter, John and Sally's new understanding of their personalities led to a productive compromise they could both feel good about: they decided that Sally could plan one social function for them to participate in as a couple each weekend. Sally agreed to make sure to leave one weekend day or night for John to have plenty of downtime to recharge in the ways he preferred.

PERSONALITY STRENGTHS OF HAPPY COUPLES

Our past research has shown that there are specific personality traits that predictably damage couple relationships; the absence of these traits, on the other hand, opens the door to intimacy. In our study of fifty thousand couples, personality was found to be a powerful discriminator between happy and unhappy couples. When negative personality traits (i.e., withdrawn, moody, and controlling) become chronically out of balance, they are like a toxic poison to your relationship. Figure 11.1 demonstrates how happy couples report significantly lower rates of these negative and out-of-balance traits in their partners than do unhappy couples.

FIGURE 11.1
Strengths of Happy Couples verses Unhappy Couples
Regarding Personality Issues

Personality Issue	Percentage in Agreement	
	Happy Couples	Unhappy Couples
1. My partner is often unhappy or withdrawn.	41%	86%
2. My partner is unreliable and doesn't follow through.	16%	75%
3. My partner is too controlling.	30%	88%

4. My partner's behavior is embarrassing or upsetting.	29%	75%
5. It is difficult to deal with my partner's moodiness.	47%	85%

We highly recommend you take an honest look in the mirror and take an inventory of yourself. If you display any of these traits on a consistent basis, give careful consideration to how you might harness them and find more balance in the future. Strive to rid yourself of such things and clothe yourself with kindness, humility, flexibility, and self-control.

SCOPE AND THE BIG FIVE

The Couple Checkup includes a personality section called SCOPE, which is an acronym for Social, Change, Organized, Pleasing, and Emotionally Steady. It is based on what is often considered to be the most robust and highly researched model of personality in the world of psychology, the Five Factor Model.[3] Unlike other personality assessments, which are driven by a theoretical model of how personality is organized, the Five Factor Model began with no theory in mind. Instead, researchers conducted a statistical analysis of every adjective in the English language to see what patterns or "factors" emerged. The resulting five factors have now been replicated in many other languages and cultures.

The SCOPE categories are designed to be positive and easy to understand. Figure 11.2 provides an overview of what a high score means on each SCOPE category. Unlike some other personality scales, it is possible to get all high or all low scores on the five areas. In other words, each of the traits is relatively independent of one another. The following section describes high, average, and low scores in each area.

FIGURE 11.2
SCOPE Personality Profile Categories

Social	Change	Organized	Pleasing	Emotionally Steady
Extroverted vs. Introverted	Open to Change vs. Conventional	Conscientious vs. Less Organized	Agreeable vs. Forceful	Calm vs. Reactive
Skilled in handling social situations	Prefers variety to routine	Always prepared	Respects others	Not easily bothered by things
The life of the party	Likes to begin new things	Makes plans and sticks with them	Doesn't like to be pushy	Seldom gets mad
Comfortable around people	Enjoys visiting new places	Carries out plans	Believes in the good intentions of others	Rarely complains
Makes friends easily	Values flexibility	Seldom wastes time	Accepts people as they are	Seldom feels blue
Often on the go	Enjoys thinking of new ways to do things	Gets chores and tasks done right away	Values cooperation over competition	Comfortable in unfamiliar situations
Loves large parties	Comfortable with change	Likes order	Loves to help others	Feels comfortable with self
Doesn't mind being the center of attention		Tries to follow the rules	Has a good word for everyone	Remains calm under pressure

Social

The Social trait considers one's behavior in regard to social situations.

High Social Scores: Those who score high on this scale are more extroverted. They enjoy being with people and are often full of energy. Such individuals tend to be enthusiastic and action oriented. In groups, they like to talk, assert themselves, and often be the center of attention. When out of balance, they can appear to be seeking attention or shallow. Others may even see high extroversion as an inability to take life seriously.

If both you and your partner score high on the Social scale, you are likely a very outgoing and energetic couple, poised for lots of fun. People are likely drawn to you because of your fun-loving mind-set and ability to make friends easily. Potential drawbacks include becoming overly busy or too involved in outside activities. You may neglect placing enough priority on your couple relationship due to your busy social calendar. When out of balance, this leaves less time for your personal life and couple relationship. You may benefit from periodically scheduling time to reconnect alone with your partner.

Average Social Scores: Those who score in the average range may find social settings enjoyable, but will value privacy as well. Their preference for being in groups or alone may change based on their mood or external circumstances. Couples who both score in this range generally enjoy having a balance between alone time and social activity.

Low Social Scores: Those who score low on the Social scale tend to be reserved or introverted. Social introverts often lack the exuberance and activity levels of extroverts. They tend to be low key, deliberate, and less connected socially. They often prefer to be alone or with just a few close friends. They will feel more energized after spending time alone or in small, intimate settings, as opposed to in large groups or parties. When out of balance, they appear reclusive or cut off from others. Some people may even misinterpret their need for personal time as aloofness.

Couples who both score low on the Social trait will be more reserved and private, enjoying quiet and relaxing time alone. Often, they do not enjoy going to large social gatherings. These events may cause more stress than enjoyment. A potential drawback is becoming isolated and cut off from others. When out of balance, two social introverts can even feel isolated from one another. They will need to find ways of connecting with one another while still allowing each other the chance to recharge alone or apart.

Handling Couple Differences: When one partner is highly social and the other is not, the couple will need to communicate openly about attending social events and getting together with others. One of them gets energy from socializing with others, while the other prefers more privacy and alone time. Unnecessary conflict can be avoided in these relationships by checking with the other partner before saying yes or no to participating in a social function.

Change

This trait reflects a person's openness to change, flexibility, and interest in new experiences.

High Change Scores: Those who score in the high range are more flexible, unconventional, and open to new experiences. They often have a broad range of interests. Such individuals thrive on coming up with new and creative solutions to problems, even when a tried-and-true method might work just as well. When out of balance, they may appear to be overly interested in new ideas and adventures, forgetting more practical realities.

Couples who both score high on this dimension are likely to enjoy change in their lives. They sometimes need to be careful to not create too much change leading to unnecessary stress in their lives. Remember that the practical or conventional approach is sometimes the tried-and-true method, worthy of sticking with.

Average Change Scores: Those in the average range often strike a good balance between new, abstract, or creative ideas and more traditional or down-to-earth approaches to life. Based on the situations they encounter, they may fluctuate between being flexible or taking a business-as-usual approach. Couples who both score in the average range are often practical but still open to considering new ideas when appropriate.

Low Change Scores: Individuals with low Change scores are more down to earth, practical in nature, and less interested in new ideas and experiences. Change may be difficult for them and increase their stress levels. They prefer the familiar approaches they already understand and are accustomed to. Attitudes are likely to be more conventional or traditional. When out of balance, these individuals can appear rigid or closed off to new experiences.

Couples who both score low in Change will present themselves as practical and more conventional in their attitudes. Neither person will rock the boat or create unnecessary stress by embracing a new approach to life. These couples may need to guard against letting their lives and relationship become too routine or boring.

Handling Couple Differences: One partner scoring higher than the other in the Change trait may represent a case of being attracted to one's opposite. The more practical person is often attracted to their partner's free-thinking and open attitudes. Conversely, the more open partner may recognize the value of his or her partner's steady approach to life. There will be times when one another's attitudes, preferences, or behavior will be challenging and may lead to frustration. Couples will need to remember to work with their differences rather than attempting to change or criticize their partner. It is helpful to look for the positives, even in very diverse approaches to the same issue.

Organized

This trait reflects how organized and determined a person is in his or her daily life and work. It also reflects persistence in pursuing goals.

High Organized Scores: Those who score high on the Organized trait are typically methodical and well organized. They tend to be persistent and reliable, placing a great deal of emphasis on this type of behavior in most areas of their life. Often quite goal oriented, they may have well-thought-out plans as they strive to achieve their goals. When out of balance, these individuals can be perceived as perfectionists, controlling, or overly driven.

Couples who both score high in organization may be very detailed and goal oriented. They will likely have the discipline to accomplish a lot of long-term goals as a couple. They value consistency and orderliness in many aspects of their life together. Potential drawbacks for couples who both score high on this dimension include becoming overly driven to achieve their goals, putting tasks before relationships. At times, their desire for consistency and planning will be challenged by unplanned stressful situations or life changes beyond their control.

Average Organized Scores: Those in the average range are generally organized. They are likely dependable and goal oriented, but they can also be flexible, setting aside work and agendas when necessary. They know how to get organized, but it is not always a high priority. While their home and workspace may be somewhat cluttered, they will still know where things are located.

Having this in common can be a positive for couples as they balance tasks, goals, and relationships. They will need to communicate with one another about areas in their life where they need to get more organized and the roles they will each fulfill to maximize their effectiveness as a couple.

Low Organized Scores: Those who score low on organization tend to resist a great deal of structure and are more spontaneous. They may also be less careful, less focused, and more likely to be distracted from tasks. Often easygoing and preferring to not make strict plans, they enjoy settings in which they are not required to conform to strict benchmarks. When out of balance, they can appear careless or disorganized.

Couples who both score low in organization will be very relaxed about plans, and neither person will place much emphasis on details. They are comfortable with a certain level of disorganization, and may wonder why some people expend so much energy focusing on minor details. Potential drawbacks for couples who both score low in organization include getting behind on routine tasks such as balancing the checking account or losing track of things such as the car keys. They need to remember that setting some goals as a couple is important, and they can find ways to compensate for less organization by strategizing in key areas of their life.

Dealing with Couple Differences: Couples with different levels of organization will need to communicate openly with one another about their goals, roles, and expectations. It is likely the once-endearing tendencies that become annoying, distracting, or even maddening when stressful events come their way. They need to find ways to balance one another and avoid the extremes of perfectionism versus sloppiness. Potential challenges include different expectations for housekeeping, relationship roles, and long-term goals. Focusing on strengths and allowing the more organized individual to handle necessary details can be helpful, but these couples will need to guard against allowing the highly organized individual to function more like a parent and less like a partner.

Pleasing

This trait reflects how considerate and cooperative a person is in his or her daily interactions with others.

High Pleasing Scores: High scores suggest a person is trusting, friendly, and cooperative. They value getting along with others and are considerate and helpful. Optimistic about people, they view others as basically honest, decent, and trustworthy. When out of balance, these individuals may sacrifice their own needs and opinions to please others. In their relationships, these people may find it difficult to ask for what they need.

Couples who both score high on this dimension will likely treat one another with a great deal of respect and consideration. They value cooperation over competition, and heated conflicts may be few and far between. They are at risk, however, of not sharing their true feelings, especially negative emotions. Stuffing opinions and feelings down can rob these relationships of deep emotional intimacy. These couples will need to learn to cultivate their assertiveness, realizing that their relationship often moves forward after sharing honestly and resolving conflict.

Average Pleasing Scores: Those with average Pleasing scores can be warm and cooperative, but occasionally somewhat competitive, stubborn, or assertive. When they feel their rights are violated, these individuals are able to respond and stand up for themselves. They generally know how to get along well with others and are well liked.

Couples who both score in this range typically know how to balance consideration for one another with assertiveness and straightforward talk.

Low Pleasing Scores: These individuals tend to be very confident, assertive, and less cooperative than those with higher scores. They can often express their anger directly and are sometimes seen as competitive and unfriendly. They are less likely to be taken advantage of and can stand up for themselves. When out of balance, they can appear skeptical, proud, or aggressive. Others can be intimidated by these individuals and find it difficult to develop a close relationship with them. These individuals may experience higher levels of conflict in their partner relationship unless they have learned how to balance their assertiveness.

Couples who both score low on the Pleasing trait will tend to be more competitive than cooperative. They have the capacity to be assertive and straightforward with one another. Potential drawbacks include conflict, debates, and the tendency to voice opinions rather than actively listen to and support one another. Their communication may be interpreted by their partners as harsh and unforgiving, rather than simply assertive. These individuals need to work on their active listening and conflict-resolution skills, as listening is often the more difficult part of communicating for them.

Dealing with Couple Differences: Couples with one partner scoring higher than the other on this dimension may need to practice their communication and conflict resolution skills. The partner scoring higher on this dimension may need to develop their ability to honestly express both positive and negative opinions and feelings. In so doing, they can allow the more assertive partner the opportunity to truly understand their feelings. The partner scoring lower on this dimension will benefit from working to be a good active listener.

Emotionally Steady

This trait reflects the tendency to stay relaxed and calm even when faced with stress.

High Emotionally Steady Scores: Those with a high score on the Emotionally Steady trait tend to be more relaxed, more calm, and less prone to distress. They are likely to be calm and emotionally stable even when confronted with stressful situations. In the extreme, they may appear unfeeling or unflappable.

Couples where both partners are Emotionally Steady remain very calm and collected as they cope with the challenges life presents. They are not prone to much distress as individuals and often handle conflict well as a couple since they are slow to become angry, anxious, or depressed.

Average Emotionally Steady Scores: Average scorers are generally calm and able to cope with stress. Others likely see them as very capable of handling everyday stressors. When under high levels of stress, they can experience negative feelings of anxiety, depression, or anger, but are generally emotionally steady and in control of their lives. Couples who both score in this range can use their communication skills, good problem solving, and flexibility to help them navigate stressful times without the extremes of negative emotion. Focusing on what is within one's ability to influence is much more helpful than being overwhelmed by what one cannot control.

Low Emotionally Steady Scores: Those in this range are typically more emotionally sensitive and prone to becoming upset. They often have difficulty handling stress in their lives. When faced with challenges, they are prone to experience upsetting feelings such as anxiety, anger, or depression. When out of balance, they become emotionally fragile or overly sensitive. Some acquaintances may see these emotional reactions as difficult to handle and pull away from the relationship, leaving these individuals feeling isolated.

Couples who both score in this range know what it feels like to be stressed and in a bad mood. They should be able to understand and empathize when their partner is feeling anxious, down, or angry. Their individual moods, however, can impact the couple relationship as well. They need to be mindful of how much anxiety, change, and stress they can each handle. Being understanding listeners and supportive partners during times of stress will maximize their ability to weather life's challenges together.

Dealing with Couple Differences: Couples with one partner scoring higher than the other may experience occasional challenges. In times of stress, the more emotionally calm partner may need to take control and help the other person feel less frustrated. The one experiencing anxiety, anger, or sadness might wonder why their partner doesn't feel the same way. It is helpful for these couples to remember to work with one another's differences rather than attempt to change or criticize their partner.

REMEMBER WHAT YOU WERE ATTRACTED TO?

Sometimes the very thing you were attracted to in the beginning of a relationship begins to annoy or bother you later on:

- She married him because he was such an assertive male; she later disliked that he was such a domineering husband.

- He married her because she was so gentle and petite; he later disliked that she was so weak and helpless.

- She married him because he had goals and could provide a good income; she later disliked that all he did was work.

- He married her because she was so quiet and dependent; he later disliked that she was so boring and clingy.
- She married him because he was the life of the party; she later disliked that he couldn't enjoy an evening at home.
- He married her because she was so neat and organized; he later disliked that she was so compulsive and controlling.

It is easy to forget the positive aspects of your partner's personality and begin to focus only on the negative aspects of each trait. But try to remember that something in that annoyance was attractive to you at one point; perhaps because that trait completes you or blesses you in some way.

It took awhile but John and Sally eventually learned to accept and cele-brate one another's personality differences. Once again John appreciated Sally's friendships and how she helped him engage with others socially. Sally discov-ered value in setting goals in life and pursuing them with her husband. But perhaps most importantly, both John and Sally learned to not take it personally when the other pursued their personal interests. John didn't feel guilty when Sally spent time with her friends, and Sally didn't feel neglected when John opted to "sit this one out" and stay home. Each learned to give . . . and receive . . . and celebrate. For a time they thought they had married the wrong person, but they eventually discovered that they had married the right person.

YOU ALWAYS MARRY THE WRONG PERSON

> You didn't really know
> what you thought you knew
> when you did what you did
> and said what you said.
> You didn't know what you needed
> or what you needed to know
> to choose who you chose
> so you can't see what you saw.

YOU ALWAYS MARRY THE RIGHT PERSON

Although you didn't really know
what you thought you knew,
you really did know
what you needed to know
when you did what you did.
You knew more than you knew,
you did better than you would
had you known what you didn't.[4]

CHECK-IN PROCESS

Where are you *now*? (Identify and discuss your results.)

1. In what areas are your personalities similar?

_____

_____

How might the similarities affect your relationship positively?

_____

_____

Are there any drawbacks to being alike in these areas? (e.g., both scoring low on organization)

_____

_____

2. Review the following negative personality traits. With which ones might you have a problem?

   Moodiness. Critical or negative attitude. Controlling. Depressed or withdrawn. Stubborn. Temperamental. Unreliable.

   How might you help one another rid yourselves of these challenges?

_____

_____

3. Review the Couple Checkup Results.

   In what areas are your personalities different?

_____

_____

How might the differences impact your relationship, both positively and negatively?

_____

_____

To what degree have you come to accept your spouse's personality? What still remains difficult to celebrate?

_____

_____

Do the roles you are expected to fulfill in your relationship match your personality strengths? (e.g., Is an individual who scores low on organization being asked to manage the checkbook?)

Where would you like to be? (Discuss issues.)
1. Choose one personality difference or negative personality trait that you both want to resolve or change.
2. Share how you each feel about this difference or trait.
3. What would you do differently if you could accept or celebrate this difference more often, or what behavior would you implement to decrease the presence of the negative trait?

How do you get there? (Develop your action plan.)
1. Brainstorm a list of ways to handle your personality problems.
2. Agree on one solution you will try.
3. Decide what you will each do to make the plan work.
4. Review the progress in one week.

COUPLE EXERCISE 11.1
SCOPE Personality Scale

1. Rate yourself as high, medium, or low on the five personality areas in SCOPE.

2. Next, rate how you view your partner in the same areas.

	High	Medium	Low
S – Social			
C – Change			
O – Organized			
P – Pleasing			
E – Emotionally Steady			

COUPLE DISCUSSION

- Compare and discuss how you rated yourselves.
- Compare and discuss how you rated one another.
- If you have taken your Couple Checkup, compare the results from this exercise with your Checkup report.

REMINDERS FOR DEALING
WITH PERSONALITY DIFFERENCES

1. Don't try to change your partner's personality. It won't work!

2. Be responsible for yourself. The fact that personality traits are generally pervasive throughout life does not give you an excuse to not learn behaviors that will positively contribute to your marriage. For example, in order to serve your spouse you can learn to pick up after yourself even though a mess in the kitchen or dirty clothes on the floor doesn't bother you.

3. Remember the positive aspects of your partner's personality that attracted you to him or her in the first place.

4. Consider where you may be out of balance in your own personality and behavior. Think of strategies that could bring more balance to your life.

5. Use your self-awareness to comment out loud on what you're doing and why you're doing it. For example, you might say, "I know it's a little hard to talk to me this evening. I'm very concerned about a deadline at work, and with my personality, I always get a little more focused, quiet, and hard to reach when something's on my mind. Please know it's not about you. We're OK. I just need to get through this deadline, OK?"

TWELVE

ACHIEVING YOUR GOALS

The most powerful weapon on earth is the human soul on fire.

—MARSHALL FERDINAND FOCH (1851–1929)

WHAT DO YOU HOPE FOR?

There is an old saying that defines three things we need in life: something to do, something to love, and something to hope for. "Something to do" provides structure to our days, "something to love" provides meaning, and "something to hope for" provides optimism. Without some kind of structure to our days, we can still function, but not very well, particularly during difficult times. What and who we love and value are where most people derive real meaning for their existence. Hope allows us to anticipate something positive, even in the face of hardship.

We all need hopes and dreams for the future, and one way these become observable is through goals. Goals provide direction and give hope for the future. Studies have found that individuals with written goals tend to have better health and happier marriages than those without goals. Discussing and sharing goals facilitates closeness, emotional bonding, and goal achievement.

COMMON OBSTACLES TO ACHIEVING GOALS

There are so many ways you can fail to achieve your goals. We want to point out some of the common ones so that you can avoid these mistakes and, thereby, be more successful. Here are some of the most common reasons why couples do not achieve their goals: lacking awareness of each other's goals, having conflicting goals, unequal motivation to achieve their goals, negative thinking, procrastination, and unrealistic goals. So try to avoid these obstacles.

Lack of Awareness of Each Other's Goals

Sometimes what is interpreted as lack of support for a partner's goals is really just lack of awareness. For example, you may be trying to lose weight and may feel that your partner is sabotaging your diet by eating tempting foods in front of you. But if you talk with your partner about your goals and desires—in this case, to lose weight—he or she will be better able to encourage and support you, and vice versa. Studies have shown that couple support is one of the more powerful ways to help change negative health behaviors or recover from illness.

Conflicting Goals and Unequal Motivation

At times one partner's personal goal may interfere with a couple or family goal. For example, one partner may want to go back to work full-time, which means they will not be as available to care for the children, prepare meals, and do household chores. Or one partner may want to go back to school while the other wants to start saving for the children's college. These two goals are potentially very conflicting and can cause tension in the family and couple relationship.

Sometimes one partner is more motivated to change than the other. This can occur for a multitude of reasons. If you are the highly motivated partner, don't try to nag your spouse into becoming motivated. It doesn't work. In fact, it usually pushes him or her farther away from change. Focus instead on yourself and changing your part of the relationship dance. Family therapists have long known that if one person changes in a relationship, the relationship changes as well. The tango is a two-person dance. If you decide to do the waltz instead, it will not make sense for your partner to keep doing the tango.

Negative Thinking

It is not your actual circumstances that cause your emotions but your thoughts or attitudes about those circumstances. And you have total control over your thoughts and attitudes. As Henry Ford wittily observed, "Whether you think you can or whether you think you can't, you're right."[1] So, although you cannot control your emotions, you can learn to choose the thoughts that produce them.

Many people make the mistake of telling themselves they can't do something. With a "can't" attitude, you simply set yourself up for failure—failure that usually has nothing to do with ability and everything to do with willingness. *Can't* almost always means *won't*. From now on, when the word *can't* seeps into your mind, think about it as an acronym: Can After Numerous Tries.

When you change your thinking, you can change your life. Here's how:

When you change your thinking, you change your beliefs.
When you change your beliefs, you change your expectations.
When you change your expectations, you change your attitude.
When you change your attitude, you change your behavior.
When you change your behavior, you change your performance.
When you change your performance, you change your life.

—Anonymous

Procrastination

Woody Allen once said, "Seventy percent of success in life is showing up."[2] Although this sounds simplistic, if you think about it, you'll realize that it makes sense. As a working person, the most difficult part of your day is likely right after waking, when you have to motivate yourself to actually get out of bed and get ready to go to work.

As a runner who has trained for and run a marathon, I (Amy) can testify that the hardest part of those training runs was feeling motivated enough to put on my running shoes. Once I was running, I was happy to be doing it. And afterward I usually felt exhilarated, fulfilled, and renewed. We all know that half the battle is simply getting started. Once you start something, you will be into it. Don't hold back. Now is the most important time in your life. What are you waiting for?

It takes a tremendous amount of energy to procrastinate. As William James pointed out, "Nothing is so fatiguing as the eternal hanging on of an uncomplicated task."[3] Use that energy—don't waste it.

Unrealistic Goals

> "Many of us are afraid to follow our passions, to pursue what we want most because it means taking risks and even facing failure. But to pursue your passion with all your heart and soul is success in itself. The greatest failure is to have never really tried."
>
> ROBYN ALLAN

The idea of having unrealistic goals occurs on two levels. The first level is in having goals that are not attainable because they are based on unreasonable logic or resources. An illogical goal would be, "I want to never disagree with my spouse again." The impracticality of this goal renders it useless. On the other hand, a couple could certainly create a specific goal related to arguing that is within reach, such as, "I want to never again shut down emotionally when we fight." And then have strategies in place to prevent that from happening.

The second level of unrealism in goals has to do with having an unrealistic frame of reference to measure our goals. Advertising and the media have played important roles in altering our standards of what we want and what we value. We need to be aware of whether or not the illusory market-made images have insidiously become our own goals. If these are our measures we will inevitably fail, because we are using an artificial system to dictate the direction of our lives. External things can provide some comfort and occasional distraction, but fulfillment is an internal journey. Anytime an external frame of reference is used to measure our lives, the goals that arise from there will not reflect our inner being.

Obstacles to Overcome

We often get in our own way when it comes to achieving goals, as most of the obstacles so far reflect—procrastinating, thinking negatively, or impracticality. But other times there are genuine obstacles that need to be addressed: resources (such as time and money) needed, education required, a certain set of skills to be learned. If your goals are realistic, decisions and actions can be made and implemented.

Defining and attaining goals is not always easy, but it is not supposed to be. We have to expect obstacles, delays, and disappointments. But the challenges associated with setting and achieving goals make the rewards that much more fulfilling.

SUGGESTIONS FOR ACHIEVING GOALS

Be Authentic

Being yourself is a prerequisite to getting what you really want. Authenticity is expressed when your behavior and speech resonates with your inner being; it is an honest expression of your inner values. If you show up to a relationship being inauthentic, no one will have the opportunity to respond to your authentic self. All the feedback you receive will be based on the self you *display*, rather than the self you *are*. Consequently, the outcome can never be what you really wish for except by pure chance. The following is an example of two people who came together by eliminating pieces of themselves in order to make a connection:

Paul and Julie met in college when they were each nineteen years old. Paul was a skilled athlete and played football and basketball for their college. It was on the basketball court where Paul first caught Julie's eye, although they knew one another casually through mutual friends. Julie was not the sports fan that Paul was, but it was college and so quite normal for students to attend sporting events in support of the school and the players. Even before they started dating, Julie loved to watch Paul on the basketball court; he was a dynamic player and one of their school's best.

While Paul's passion was sports, Julie's passion was in the natural world. Julie's family instilled an appreciation of nature in her and her siblings. Her parents owned a lake home in northern

Minnesota, where there were plenty of ways to enjoy the outdoors year-round, such as hiking, gardening, canoeing, cross-country skiing, or fishing. Paul was raised strictly in the city, which is where he felt most comfortable. In the years of their courtship it felt easy for Julie to attend Paul's sporting events and likewise easy for Paul to tolerate visits to the lake home of Julie's family.

It was only after they were married that Julie described Paul's interest in sports as "fanatical" and Paul began to complain about the trips to the lake home. Julie explains, "We never get a break from these stupid sports he watches—it is football in the fall, basketball in the winter, baseball in the spring and summer. I feel as though Paul is married to his sports teams, not to me and the children."

Paul's disdain for the cabin is confounded by the fact that Julie's family has always chosen to not have a television there so that they can concentrate on being together and enjoying the simplicity and sounds of nature. He never wants to join the family at the lake home, and when he does, he complains to Julie about missing televised sporting events, as well as about the mosquitoes and other bugs, boredom, and not wanting to participate in any activities there.

They each feel as though they were hoodwinked. Paul explains, "When we first met, Julie loved sports as much as I do; she used to even go to live games. Now she won't even sit on the sofa with me and watch one." Julie feels equally deceived. "Paul seemed to really enjoy our times at the lake home when we were dating. He even went ice fishing with my brothers! Now he says that life at the lake home is 'uncivilized.' I don't even like it when he comes because I know he is not having fun. On the other hand, I want our children to learn to appreciate nature, and the lake home is where extended family go to be together."

While Paul and Julie did not intentionally deceive one another, their eager participation in these activities during the dating phase led the other to believe that it would continue. They were not being authentic to themselves, which ultimately set up problems for their future. The groundwork for settling on goals is to live authentically within your interests, desires, and needs.

Look Inward—Rather than to Others—for Your Value

It is true that our relationships enrich and sustain us, but we need to begin with ourselves—coming to the relationship enriched and sustained on our own. If we were to peer inside unhappy relationships, we would probably find unhappy individuals. How can we expect to be happy as a couple if we are not happy as individuals?

We must feel whole and complete in order to offer anything substantial in a relationship. You cannot give away what you don't have. Perhaps this is why there is a correlation between age of marriage and divorce rates. Younger people have not had the time to know themselves—they often experiment with different "selves" as part of discovering their values.

> "We don't see things as they are; we see things as we are."
>
> ANAÏS NIN

Each of us has inherent value that cannot be changed by time or circumstance. Tapping into this peace and understanding helps us create better relationships. What you often see, though, are people who look to external sources for their own value. Some of these sources are material possessions, success, status in society, and physical beauty. These diversions are obstacles to personal growth and authentic living, but they are also obstacles to reaching goals.

When the intention behind a goal is to enhance your image, the goal is not pure and the result may not be what you intend. For example, if you are a businessperson and your goal is only to make money, you are not setting yourself up for success. On the other hand, if your goal is total customer satisfaction, then the by-product will be financial success. If you are a student and your goal is only to get an A, you may or may not achieve that goal. But if your goal is knowledge, then the by-product will be a good grade.

Define and Prioritize Goals

Often we do not take time to reflect on our goals. Rather, we follow routines. It is easy to go through each day and not challenge yourself to try new things. But you need to be more proactive than reactive in terms of your goals; you need focus and direction. Defining your goals enables you to envision and strive toward them. It also helps you gain a sense of progress as you accomplish them. In Couple Exercise 12.1, you will have the chance to list and prioritize your goals.

Once you have determined what it is you want, you need to prioritize goals and examine the aspects of your life that may be affected by them. What is most important to you? On what are you not willing to compromise? For example, if you have a goal of saving for a family vacation, and you have the option of working overtime to earn extra money, you may need to evaluate how much time you will spend away from your family working overtime. If you determine that the cost of less family time for several months is too high a price to pay, then you may need to consider other ways of saving money or alternative family vacation plans.

Completing this exercise with your partner designates goals as joint efforts. Rather than a me-push-you-pull struggle, you become united as teammates with a common objective.

Visualize Goals

It is human nature for us to become what we think. For example, if you think of yourself as being lazy, you will act lazy; if you think of yourself as being friendly, you will act friendly. Once you define your goals, you need to focus on and visualize them. Albert Einstein, one of the master problem solvers of all time, knew the value of visualization: "Imagination is everything. It is the preview of life's coming attraction."[4]

I (Amy) know a woman who exudes generosity and kindness to others but has been in a long-term relationship where little giving exists. The relationship has become so depleted that they do not even go on dates anymore. She once told me, "I can't even *imagine* having a man take me to dinner." My response was, "That is part of the problem." How can she co-create something she cannot even visualize herself?

Visualization is the first step to actualization. Create a mental picture of your goal in action. You know what it is you want to do. You want to vacation in Australia? Imagine yourself exploring the Great Barrier Reef, climbing Ayers Rock, and eating shrimp off the *barbie*. You want to strengthen your relationship with your partner? Imagine taking a class together, having enjoyable conversations, and laughing out loud as you walk hand in hand. You want more education? Imagine yourself sitting in a classroom listening to a lecture or sitting in the library reading something that stimu-

> "Whatever you can do or dream you can do, you can. Boldness has a genius, magic and power to it."
>
> JOHANN GOETHE

lates, challenges, and excites you. You want to fit into all the clothes in your closet again? Visualize yourself in the physical condition you desire. Hold that thought in your mind, and do what you need to do every day to bring yourself one day closer to your goals. The perceptual process is our habitual way of looking at the world. We become what holds our attention.

"Fall Down Seven Times, Get Up Eight"

Have you ever noticed that the lives of people who have achieved their dreams are filled with numerous past "failures"? Why is that? They do not let disappointments define them. These people are persistent; they persevere. They continue trying because they know "mistakes" are simply a part of the journey to success. For example, if you have ever watched babies learning to walk, you will have noticed that they continuously pull themselves up, fall down, pull themselves up again, take a step or two, fall down, and so on. They are living what is expressed in the Japanese proverb, "Fall down seven times, get up eight."

The noted sports psychologist and motivational speaker Dr. Rob Gilbert often points out, "Winners lose more than losers lose."[5] What exactly does this mean? On one of his Success Hotline messages, he offers the following Autobiography of a Loser: "I have missed more than nine thousand shots in my career. I have lost almost three hundred games. On twenty-six occasions I had to take the game-winning shot and I missed. And I failed over and over and over again in my life—that is precisely why I succeed." These are the words of Michael Jordan, possibly the greatest basketball player of all time. So, winners lose more than losers lose because winners make more attempts than losers.

As the actress Mary Pickford observed: "If you have made mistakes, there is always another chance for you. You may have a fresh start any moment you choose, for this thing we call 'failure' is not the falling down, but the staying down."[6]

Don't be afraid to make mistakes. Mistakes give you an opportunity to examine behaviors and habits and to understand the connection between new actions and new outcomes. To stop making mistakes is to also stop learning, growing, and improving. People who aren't making mistakes are on a detour from the road to success and improvement, and that is a bigger mistake.

One Step at a Time

> "The journey of a thousand miles begins with a single step."
>
> CHINESE PROVERB

Instead of thinking in terms of the "big picture," break your goal down into small, bite-size chunks. If you wanted to run a marathon, you wouldn't just go out and run one. You might start out jogging a mile or two at a time, and then gradually increase your distance.

Similarly, if you want to improve your relationship with your partner, remember that it is the small things you do that make a big difference in the long run. Begin by consciously complimenting your partner at least one additional time each day. Show that you care by making eye contact and really listening. Be generous with hugs, kisses, and caresses. Send a no-occasion card to your home or your partner's workplace. Or simply pay attention to something your partner enjoys and surprise him or her with that "something."

Think about and work toward your goal every day. Be aware of the small steps you can take to bring you closer to your goal. Ask yourself, "Is what I'm doing right now getting me closer to my goal?" "Are these cookies getting me closer to my goal of weight loss?" "Are my criticisms of my spouse bringing me closer to my goal of a fulfilling marriage?" "Is this the best use of my time right now?"

Gratitude

Gratitude is so powerful because it forces us to be in the present moment by appreciating the immediate experience of reality. One of the most powerful and transformative experiences I (Amy) have ever had was in creating a Gratitude Journal. The idea has been written about quite a bit, and I can testify that it works! I began a gratitude journal during a time in my life that felt rather bleak. I was staying home with my youngest child, which could have been great except that I didn't have social structures in place to deal with the change and newfound free time. I had given up a long friendship that wasn't healthy; one of my best friends had moved twelve hundred miles away; I wasn't working and didn't have a plan for reentering the workforce; I had no structure to my days—no goals or meetings; and I had taken a sojourn from running, which had been a form of active meditation for me since I was a teenager. Overall I was mentally and emotionally unenthused, except by my colicky baby girl!

As I began my gratitude journal, I was afraid I would have little to write about. My plan was simply to write five things every day for which I was grateful, relating to that day or current moment in time. Initially this took some deliberation because, as I only realized later, I was experiencing depression. From the vantage point of my current life (seven years later), it seems to be a simple task, and today I feel as though I could list five things every five seconds for which I am grateful. But at that time I remember sitting on the edge of my bed with the blank page in front of me, making an effort to find five things for which to be grateful.

Here are items from the first several pages from my gratitude journal:

- Pumpkin soup
- Finishing a good book . . . and anticipating another one
- Collecting rainwater for our plants
- Five hours of uninterrupted sleep
- Still having a grandma and grandpa
- Receiving a no-occasion card from Hans (my brother)

- Clean sheets

- Evan (my son) doing his homework without much of a fuss

- The sound of rain on our roof

- An appetite

I chose to write in bullet points instead of sentences. As time went by I varied the format—at times writing several paragraphs to describe an event or thought. The beginning month or two of my gratitude journal are especially precious to me because the entries were so simple, but felt so beautiful. They were not necessarily important to anyone but me.

I truly believe that this simple journal of gratitude was the beginning of a new awakening for me. This process teaches our mind to work in new ways. Acknowledging and appreciating the positive forces in our lives allows them to expand. It also becomes a natural buffer against the pattern of negative thinking. Subconsciously, we may be aware that we are on the lookout for these good forces so that we can acknowledge them later and give them credence and commemoration in the written word.

Gratefulness plays an important role in the steps needed to achieve our goals. Expressing gratitude—whether it is verbal, written, or just in thought—prepares us for achieving what we desire. We lead our minds to a positive direction into a state of highly creative motion.

TAKE ACTION

To paraphrase Mark Twain, the person who knows how to read and doesn't, has no advantage over the person who cannot read. Likewise, goals and wishes have no value until you act on them. So next time you do not "feel" like taking a step toward your goal, remember that it is the action itself that will change your state of mind, not the outcome of the action. It is not necessary for you to wait until you feel motivated. All you have to do is take the first step and the motivation will follow. The Action Plan in Couple Exercise 12.2 will help you formulate these steps.

In organizing and prioritizing goals, one of the first steps is to make certain the goal is in alignment with your principles and values and those of others in your life. Ask yourself, "Will this goal cause me to neglect the important relationships in my life?" Remember: the way you spend your time is a reflection of your priorities.

In the couple exercises that follow, you will have a chance to define personal, couple, and family goals, and then you will create an action plan for each. Thinking about personal goals as well as couple and family goals will help you balance these areas of life. Having goals in writing crystallizes them clearly before you—visually and mentally. The CHANGE model in Couple Exercise 12.2 will help you keep your goals specific and manageable, increasing the chances that your goals will be brought to fruition.

> "Coming together is a beginning; keeping together is progress; working together is success."
>
> —HENRY FORD

Keep taking "baby steps" toward your goals; these small successes will keep you motivated. Encourage your partner and work on your goals as a team. Mutual involvement in creating goals communicates to your partner that his or her dreams matter and that you will help in achieving them.

COUPLE EXERCISE 12.1
Defining Personal, Couple, and Family Goals

Clarify and define your personal, couple, and family goals for the next few years. Then share them with your partner. Remember, your goals should be realistic and clearly stated and attainable within one to five years.

Partner 1	Partner 2
Personal Goals	**Personal Goals**
1. _____	1. _____
_____	_____
2. _____	2. _____
_____	_____
3. _____	3. _____
_____	_____
Couple Goals	**Couple Goals**
1. _____	1. _____
_____	_____
2. _____	2. _____
_____	_____
3. _____	3. _____
_____	_____
Family Goals	**Family Goals**
1. _____	1. _____
_____	_____
2. _____	2. _____
_____	_____
3. _____	3. _____
_____	_____

COUPLE EXERCISE 12.2
Developing a Couple Action Plan

Once you have identified personal, couple, and family goals, we encourage you to choose one of the three areas and develop an action plan based on the CHANGE Model. The six letters in CHANGE each indicate an important step in achieving your goal. An example of how the CHANGE model can be used follows each step.

Commit yourself to a specific goal.

We will increase closeness in our marriage by spending fifteen minutes each day focusing on the positive aspects of our relationship. We will try also to go on a date one evening a week.

Habits—break old ones and start new ones.

We will set up the new routine so that the fifteen minutes falls after the evening meal each night. The evening out will usually be on Wednesday night. We will alternate who is in charge of planning the activity for the evening out.

Action—take one step at a time.

During our fifteen minutes of sharing, we will each talk about our day and our feelings about each other.

Never give up; lapses might occur.

We realize that some days we won't be able to talk for fifteen minutes about our relationship and that we won't be able to have an evening out every week, but we will do our best to stick to the plan.

Goal oriented: focus on the positive.

After our sharing, we will praise each other for taking the time and effort to connect.

Evaluate progress and reward each other.

Each Sunday night we will review the week and see how well we've done. If we have achieved our goal, we will feel pleased, and this will probably make us feel closer. If we are able to stick to this plan for six months, the final reward will be a weekend trip away together to celebrate!

CREATING YOUR ACTION PLAN

Use this as a worksheet to complete your Personal, Couple, or Family Action Plan. Writing down goals creates the road map to your success.

Commit yourselves to a specific goal.

Describe your specific goal. The more detail you give, the more clear the final outcome becomes.

_____

_____

Habits—break old ones and start new ones.

Old Habits:

_____

_____

New Plan:

_____

_____

Action—take one step at a time.

Indicate the steps in your action plan.

_____

_____

Never give up; lapses might occur.

How will you handle lapses?

_____

_____

Goal oriented: focus on the positive.

When will you praise each other?

_____

_____

Evaluate your progress and reward each other.

When will you review your progress?

_____

_____

How will you reward each other?

_____

_____

REMINDERS FOR ACHIEVING YOUR GOALS

1. Find your authentic voice. Pay attention to the origin of your goals and desires. Ask yourself: *Whose voice is talking to me? Is it my voice? My parents'? The voice of society and mass media?*

2. Decide exactly what you want. Define and share with your partner your personal, couple, and family goals.

3. Discuss with each other steps you can take to make your goals reality.

4. Start immediately. Use the CHANGE model. Make the decision, day by day, to commit to the goal. Dedicate at least five minutes each day to each goal.

5. Encourage and support each other. Do not let setbacks discourage you. Recognize the valuable feedback that failure provides.

6. Start a gratitude journal. Begin noticing and documenting things for which you are grateful.

7. Never, ever give up.

8. Need motivation? Call Dr. Rob Gilbert's Success Hotline for a daily inspirational message: (973) 743-4690.

NOTES

Preface

1. Peter Kramer, *Should You Leave?* (New York: Penguin, 1997).

Chapter 1

1. Edwin H. Friedman, *The Friedman Fables* (New York: The Guilford Press, 1990).

Chapter 2

1. Robin L. Smith, *Lies at the Altar: The Truth about Great Marriages* (New York: Hyperion, 2006).

2. Linda Waite and Maggie Gallagher, *The Case for Marriage* (Cambridge, MA: Harvard University Press, 2000).

3. Benjamin Scafidi, *The Taxpayer Costs of Divorce and Unwed Childbearing* (New York, NY: Institute for American Values, 2008).

4. Waite and Gallagher, *The Case for Marriage*.

5. R. Colman and C. S. Widom, "Childhood abuse and neglect and adult intimate relationships: A prospective study," *Child Abuse and Neglect* 28, no. 11 (2004): 1133–51.

6. S. R. Aronson and A. C. Huston, "The mother-infant relationship in single, cohabiting, and married families: A case for marriage," *Journal of Family Psychology* 18, no. 1 (2004): 5–18.

7. Terrance P. Thornberry, et al, "Family Disruption and Delinquency," (bulletin, Office of Juvenile Justice and Delinquency Prevention, U.S. Department of Justice, September 1999).

8. B. J. Fowers and D. H. Olson, "Four types of premarital couples: An empirical typology based on PREPARE," *Journal of Family Psychology* 6, no. 1 (1992): 10–21.

9. David H. Olson and Amy K. Olson, *Empowering Couples* (Minneapolis, MN: Life Innovations, 2000).

10. DeMaria, Rita (2000). Distressed couples and marriage education. *Family Relations, 54,* 242–53.

11. Portia Nelson, "Autobiography in Five Short Chapters," quoted in Sark, *Inspiration Sandwich: Stories to Inspire Our Creative Freedom* (Berkeley, CA: Celestial Arts, 1992).

Chapter 3

1. John M. Gottman, Julie Schwartz Gottman, and Joan DeClaire, *10 Lessons to Transform Your Marriage* (New York: Crown Publishers, 2006).

Chapter 4

1. http://thinkexist.com/quotes/m._esther_harding.

2. Kent, Jack. *No Such Thing as a Dragon* (New York, NY: Golden Press, 1977).

3. Howard Markman, S. Stanley, and S. L. Blumberg, *Fighting for Your Marriage* (San Francisco: Jossey-Bass, 2001).

4. E. D. Eaker, L. M. Sullivan, M. Kelly-Hayes, R. B. D'Agostino, and E. J. Benjamin, "Marital status, marital strain, and risk of coronary heart disease or total mortality: The Framingham Offspring Study," *Psychosomatic Medicine* 69, no. 6 (2007): 509–13.

5. Miriam Greenspan, "Healing through the world's hurt," *Ode Magazine* (April 2003).

Chapter 5

1. P. R. Amato and S. J. Rogers, "A longitudinal study of marital problems and subsequent divorce," *Journal of Marriage and the Family* 59 (2007): 612–24.

2. M. A. Whisman, A. E. Dixon, and B. Johnson, "Therapists' perspectives of couple problems and treatment issues in couple therapy," *Journal of Family Psychology* 11, no. 3 (1997): 361–66.

3. Juliet B. Schor, *The Overspent American* (New York: HarperPerennial, 1998).

4. Tim Kasser, and Allen D. Kanner, *Psychology and Consumer Culture: The Struggle for a Good Life in a Materialistic World* (Washington, DC: American Psychological Association, 2003) 45.

5. See note 1 above; L. Sanchez, and C. T. Gager, "Hard living, perceived entitlement to a great marriage, and marital dissolution," *Journal of Marriage and Family* 63 (2000): 708–22; D. R. Johnson and A. Booth, "Rural economic decline and marital quality: A panel study of farm marriages," *Family Relations* 39, no. 2 (1990): 159–65.

6. R. M. Ryan and E. L. Deci, "On happiness and human potentials: A review of research on hedonic and eudiamonic well-being," *Annual Review of Psychology* 52 (2001): 141–66.

7. Tim Kasser, *The High Price of Materialism* (Cambridge, MA: MIT Press, 2002).

8. Miriam Arond and Samuel L. Pauker, *The First Year of Marriage* (New York: Warner, 1987).

9. Frances Sue Anthony and Wayne Anthony, "Money and Marriage: Having both . . . happily ever after," (lecture, Columbus, Georgia, July 2007).

10. B. Bartlett, "Americans scorn class envy," FindArticles.com (June 9, 2000), http://findarticles.com/p/articles/mi-qu3827/is (accessed November 1, 2007).

Chapter 6

1. Philip W. Blumstein and Pepper Schwartz, *American Couples* (New York: Morrow, 1983).

2. Jean Kilbourne, *Deadly Persuasion: Why Women and Girls Must Fight the Addictive Power of Advertising* (New York: The Free Press, 1999).

3. The Center of Media and Public Affairs Study, "New Look at TV Sex and Violence," *National Catholic Register* (April 2000): 16–22.

4. David Buckingham and Sarah Bragg, *Young People, Sex and the Media: The Facts of Life* (New York: Palgrave Macmillan, 2004).

5. Anne Moir and David Jessel, *Brain Sex* (New York: Delta Publishing, 1991).

6. Ibid.

7. Rob Gilbert, ed., *Bits and Pieces* (Fairfield, NJ: The Economics Press, 1997).

8. Gary Chapman, *The Five Love Languages* (Chicago, IL: Northfield Publishing, 1995).

9. James Sheridan, *A Blessing for the Heart* (Adrian, MI: Marriage Done Right, 2004) 24.

10. D. Taylor and M. Sytsma, "7 things you need to know about sex," *Christianity Today* 24, no. 2 (2007): 20.

11. L. Kolodny, "Erectile dysfunction and vascular disease: What is the connection?" *Postgrad. Medicine* 114, no. 4 (2003): 30–40.

12. David Schnarch, "Inside the sexual crucible," *Family Therapy Networker* (March/April 1993): 40–48.

13. Ibid.

14. Robert Kolodny, Virginia Johnson, and William H. Masters, *Masters and Johnson on Sex and Human Loving* (Boston: Little Brown, 1988) 452–61.

   Other:

   S. Parmet, (2004). "Male sexual dysfunction," *The Journal of the American Medical Association* 291, no. 24 (2004): 3076.

Chapter 7

1. Janice M. Steil and Beth A. Turetsky, "Is equal better? The relationship between marital equality and psychological symptomatology," *Applied Social Psychology Annual* 7 (1987): 73–97.

2. Arlie R. Hochschild, *The Second Shift* (New York: Viking, 1989).

3. Ibid.

4. James Thorton, *Chore Wars* (Berkeley, CA: Conari Press, 1997).

5. Carol Gilligan, *In a Different Voice* (Cambridge, MA: Harvard University Press, 1993).

6. Thorton, *Chore Wars.*

7. Ibid.

8. Julie Shields, *How to Avoid the Mommy Trap* (Sterling, VA: Capital Books, 2002) 127.

9. Thorton, *Chore Wars.*

   Other:

   Linda R. Hirshman, *Get to Work* (New York, NY: Viking, 2006).

   P. R. Amato, D. R. Johnson, A. Booth, and S. J. Rodgers, "Continuity and change in marital quality between 1980 and 2000," *Journal of Marriage and Family* 65, no. 1 (2003): 1–22.

Chapter 8

1. G. Gallup, Jr. (1996). Religion in America: 1996 Report. Princeton, NJ: Princeton Religion Research Center.

2. http://www.brainyquote.com/quotes/authors/m/mother_teresa.html.

3. C. Joanides, M. Mayhew, and P. M. Mamalakis, "Investigating inter-Christian and intercultural couples associated with the Greek Orthodox Archdiocese of America: A qualitative research project," *The American Journal of Family Therapy* 30 (2002): 373–83.

4. A. Booth, D. R. Johnson, A. Branaman, A. Sica, "Belief and behavior: Does religion matter?" *Journal of Marriage and Family* 57 (1995): 661–71; K. T. Sullivan, "Understanding the relationship between religiosity and marriage: An investigation of the immediate and longitudinal effects of religiosity on newlywed couples," *Journal of Family Psychology* 15 (2001): 610–26; R. R. Call-Vaughn and T. B. Heaton, "Religion's influence on marital stability," *Journal for the Scientific Study of Religion* 36, no. 3 (1997): 382–92.

5. A. Booth, D. R. Johnson, A. Branaman, A. Sica, "Belief and behavior: Does religion matter?" *Journal of Marriage and Family* 57 (1995): 661–71.

6. Froma Walsh, *Spiritual Resources in Family Therapy* (New York: Guilford Press, 1999).

7. W. E. Bock and M. L. Radelet, "The marital integration of religious independents: A reevaluation of its significance," *Review of Religious Research* 29 (1988): 228–41.

8. G. H. Brody, "Parental religiosity, family processes and youth competence in rural two-parent African-American families," *Developmental Psychology* 32, no. 4 (1996): 696–706; P. Fagan, *A Portrait of Family and Religion in America: Key Outcomes for the Common Good* (Washington, DC: The Heritage Foundation, 2006); M. D. Regnerus, C. Smith, and B. Smith, (2004). "Social context in the development of adolescent religiosity," *Applied Developmental Science* 8, no. 1 (2004): 27–38; M. Keresters, J. Youniss, and E. Metz, "Longitudinal patterns of religious perspective and civic integration," *Applied Developmental Science* 8, no. 1 (2004): 39–46; N. Kwak, D. V. Shah, and R. L. Holbert, (2004). "Connecting, trusting, and participating: The direct and interactive effects of social associations," *Political Research Quarterly* 57, no. 4 (2004): 643–52.

9. P. J. Larson and D. H. Olson, (2004). "Spiritual beliefs and marriage: a national survey based on ENRICH," *The Family Psychologist* 20 (2004): 2, 4–8.

10. James E. Sheridan, *A Blessing for the Heart* (Adrian, MI: Marriage Done Right, 2004) 8.

11. Froma Walsh (Editor), *Spiritual Resources in Family Therapy* (New York: Guilford Press, 1999).

12. Don Miguel Ruiz, *The Four Agreements: 2001 Engagement Calendar for Wisdom and Personal Freedom* (New York: Andrews McMeel, 2001) 2.

13. Krista Tippett, *Speaking of Faith* (New York, NY: Viking, 2007) 3.

14. http://thinkexist.com/quotes/mother_teresa/.

15. http://www.brainyquote.com/quotes/authors/m/martin_luther_king_jr.html.

16. http://www.brainyquote.com/quotes/authors/m/martin_luther_king_jr.html. Other:

John Miller, Aaron Kenedi and Thomas Moore, eds., *God's Breath* (New York: Marlowe & Company, 2000).

Chapter 9

1. Kahlil Gibran, *The Prophet* (New York: Knopf, 1976) 16–17.

2. Frederick S. Perls, *Gestalt Therapy Verbatim* (Lafayette, CA: Real People Press, 1969) 4.

3. Judy Altura, "Togetherness Poem," quoted in J. Gillies, *My Needs, Your Needs* (New York: Doubleday, 1974) 20.

4. B. H. Fiese, T. J. Tomcho, M. Douglas, K. Josephs, S. Poltrock, and T. Baker, "A review of fifty years of research on naturally occurring family routines and rituals: Cause for Celebration?" *Journal of Family Psychology* 16, no. 4 (2002).

5. David Quigley, www.alchemyinstitute.com.

Chapter 10

1. J. Inman-Amos and S. S. Hendrick, "Love attitudes: Similarities between parents and children," *Family Relations* 43 (1994).

2. BBC News, "Lifestyle fears 'hit birth rate,'" BBC News Online, http://news.bbc.co.uk/2/hi/uk_news/3270125.stm, 14 November 2003.

3. C. P. Cowan, "Becoming Parents: What has to change for couples?" quoted in C. F. Clulow, ed., *Partners Become Parents* (Northvale, NJ: Aronson, 1996).

4. Jane Brooks, *Parenting* (Mountain View, CA: McGraw-Hill, 1998).

5. Diana Baumrind, "The influence of parenting style on adolescent competence and substance abuse," *Journal of Early Adolescence* 11, no. 1 (1991) 56–95.

6. R. W. Larson, S. Wilson, B. B. Brown, F. F. Furstenberg Jr., and S. Verma, "Changes in adolescents' interpersonal experiences: Are they being prepared for adult relationships in the twenty-first century?" *Journal of Research on Adolescence* 12, no. 1 (2002) 31–68.

7. Jean Illsley Clarke, Connie Dawson, and David Bredehoft, *How Much Is Enough?* (New York: Marlowe & Company, 2004).

8. Ibid.

9. William J. Doherty, *Take Back Your Kids* (Notre Dame, IN: Sorin Books, 2000).

10. Virginia Satir, *The New Peoplemaking* (Palo Alto, CA: Science and Behavior Books, 1988).

   Other:

   N. Gibbs, "Who's in charge here?" *Time* (July 30, 2001) 40–49.

Chapter 11

1. Lawrence A. Pervin and Oliver P. John, *Personality: Theory and Research,* 8th ed. (New York: Wiley, 2001).

2. David Augsburger, *Sustaining Love* (Ventura, CA: Regal, 1988).

3. Paul Costa and Robert McCrae, *Bibliography for the Revised NEO Personality Inventory (NEO PI-R)and NEO Five-Factor Inventory (NEO-FFI)* (Lutz, FL: Psychological Assessment Resources, 2003).

4. Augsburger, *Sustaining Love*, pg. 55.

Chapter 12

1. http://quoteworld.org/quotes/4834.

2. http://www.brainyquote.com/quotes/authors/w/woody_allen-html.

3. http://www.brainyquote.com/quotes/w/william_james.html.

4. http://www.brainyquote.com/quotes/a/albert_einstein.html.

5. Dr. Rob Gilbert, *How to Have Fun without Failing Out: 430 Tips from a College Professor* (Deerfield Beach, FL: Health Communications), 2007.

6. http://www.brainyquote.com/quotes/authors/m/mary_pickford.html.

ABOUT THE AUTHORS

David H. Olson, Ph.D., is founder and CEO of Life Innovations, a thirty-year-old company with a variety of products such as the PREPARE/ENRICH program and the Couple Checkup, which are designed to build stronger marriages. A national and international marriage and family expert, Olson is professor emeritus at the University of Minnesota, where he taught for nearly thirty years, and has written more than twenty books and over one hundred articles. Dr. Olson has appeared on a variety of television shows, including *The Today Show, The Early Show, Good Morning America,* and *Oprah.*

Amy Olson-Sigg has been at Life Innovations since 1996. She has her master's in marital and family therapy and has coauthored several books, articles, and programs including PREPARE/ENRICH/Inspire for Teens (2011).

Peter J. Larson, Ph.D., has been at Life Innovations since 2004. He is a licensed clinical psychologist and has a master's degree in theology. He previously worked for several years as clinical director of the Smalley Relationship Counseling Center. Larson has written several articles on marriage and family topics and has coauthored several products and programs, including the Couple Checkup, PREPARE To Last, and the PREPARE/ENRICH program.